Recommendation Intoxication

How We Became Beguiled by an Unreliable
Workplace Habit and What We Can Do
About It

Erin Haggerty

ISBN: 1461095379
ISBN-13: 9781461095378
Library of Congress Control Number: 2011906113

For Max
My favorite co-worker

Table of Contents

Chapter One

An Acid-Filled Syringe

Doctors and nurses en route to work at Vanderbilt Hospital in Nashville, Tennessee, were expecting a typical day of broken arms, earaches, and heart attacks. Little did they anticipate the bizarre event that would alter this routine.

Vanderbilt overlooks a parking lot where Dr. George Allen, a renowned neurosurgeon, had a parking space reserved for his use.

But on this particular day, Allen's parking space was occupied by a visitor who appeared to have unusual intentions. That visitor was Dr. Ray Mettetal, Allen's former employee. However, Mettetal did not look his usual self. In fact, he had donned a wig, a fake beard, and body padding. In his hand, he held a large syringe filled with a boric acid solution, which police believed he planned to inject into Allen. An observant hospital employee, however, alerted authorities, who arrested Mettetal in the parking lot.

Upon investigation, the police discovered a variety of activities that they found questionable. For example, Mettetal, using a fake name, had traveled to Tennessee from

Virginia and had shadowed Allen over a period of time. Moreover, interest in the case spread beyond the local police force to the U.S. Secret Service. This happened because Allen had performed brain surgery on Al Gore's mother during Gore's vice presidency, and the U.S. Secret Service observed the investigation out of concern for national security.

After serving more than seven years in prison, Mettetal was acquitted and released after the courts determined his original arrest was illegal. Following his release, Mettetal satisfied psychological fitness requirements, and both his Virginia and Tennessee medical licenses were reinstated.

But what could possibly drive Mettetal, a doctor with a presumably bright professional future, or *any* person to behave in such a manner?

This astonishing action was caused by the absence of a piece of paper—a *letter of recommendation*. Back in 1984, when Mettetal worked at Vanderbilt, Allen reportedly refused to give Mettetal a recommendation to forward his career. The absence of this endorsement set in motion a chain of events that snowballed over the course of a decade.[1]

Is the Mettetal-Allen saga just another breaking news story or does it have ramifications that reach far beyond the Vanderbilt Hospital parking lot?

Indeed, the ramifications are far reaching. This book alerts employers, employees, and students to the pitfalls of *letters of recommendation* and the impact they have on our business culture and professional lives. From first job to retirement, baby boomers to millennials, people connected to the workplace participate in this system of assessment. Employees request letters, supervisors provide them, and the workplace seemingly thrives. Unfortunately, most of us do not question this system of assessment—but we should.

Everyone, from CEO to recent college grad, who dares to look beneath the surface of the recommendation story, will find an unreliable assessment system that encourages a dangerous dependency on faulty information. Even so, many people feel uneasy about openly challenging the system. But behind closed doors, people express concern that challenging the system would put their job prospects and promotions at risk. Further, they fear being labeled by the workplace as fools who do not understand the importance of recommendations, as hysterics who are making a big deal out of a small matter, or as professional miscreants who have something to hide.

Still, many people have an intuitive sense that the recommendation system is not a valid form of assessment, but rather a tool that allows a select few people to control the lives of others through seduction or threat. This reality is revealed clearly and poignantly through the stories people tell about the use of recommendations in the work and academic worlds. As the Mettetal-Allen saga demonstrates in dramatic fashion, people are quite serious about the assessment of their professionalism. People feel the power of the recommendation system in a deeply personal way.

Why?

It's a matter of competition and opportunity. The recommendation tradition is a gatekeeping system that determines who will move ahead in the workplace race and who will be left in the dust. Small wonder that the recommendation system, used to empower or to derail business and individual success, inspires reactions ranging from elation to extreme anger.

Still, we behave as if recommendations are an essential part of a well-functioning business culture.

But *why* do we behave this way?

The answer may lie in our own heads. Science has determined that the human brain is hardwired to develop addictions to behaviors that sustain social bonds. When people engage in such behaviors, the brain generates an intoxicating surge of "feel good" chemicals that lead people to repeat the behavior. One example of such a behavior is the human search for information.

Gossip is an example of one type of intoxicating information that people seek. Gossip is popular because it is useful for maintaining social bonds that help people avoid dangerous situations and locate life-sustaining opportunities.

But why do we like gossip so much, and what does this behavior have to do with recommendations?

The popular online social networking site Twitter may contain the answer to this question. Psychologists and scientists who study the human brain have become interested in what happens inside the brain when people engage in gossip through social forums such as Twitter. Twitter is an online network in which people can send messages known as "tweets" to each other throughout the day. Typically a tweet contains daily gossip—information about the daily occurrences happening in the life of the tweet sender.

A typical tweet might say "Just finished grocery shopping and found peaches on sale." Psychologists have presented the idea that the mega success of Twitter may be based on the fact that Twitter technology allows people to continuously experience the surge of "feel good" chemicals released when people gossip.[2]

In short, "tweeting" gives us a buzz. If true, Twitter capitalizes on our tendency to seek interactions that strengthen our social bonds by feeding our gossip addiction twenty-four hours a day seven days a week.

Gossip, in "tweets" or other formats, is important because gossip is a type of information, and we are an information-based society and workplace. In the workplace, we rightly tend to regard information as positive and empowering. But there's a catch. While information has the power to inform, it also has the power to beguile and intoxicate.

How does information intoxicate?

Intoxication occurs whenever we consume something—alcohol, sex, or *information*—to such an extent or in such a manner that we are no longer in control and our ability to make well-reasoned decisions becomes impaired. A state of intoxication can make us feel more confident and more in control. However, intoxication is not real control, but merely a beguiling illusion.

So what does gossip and information intoxication have to do with the use of recommendations in the workplace?

Everything. The workplace is not immune to information intoxication. The workplace is especially intoxicated on the information exchanged about *people* in the form of gossip. While daily gossip is spread through forums such as Twitter, professional gossip about potential employees is traded in the workplace through recommendations. The stories in this book show how the workplace has become intoxicated from the habitual consumption of recommendations. Moreover, the stories show how, when it comes to recommendation use, the workplace has lost control and the ability to make well-reasoned decisions, even though it behaves as if recommendations should in most situations make the workplace safer, more powerful, and more successful. Employers feel more confident and more in control when someone else can provide gossip in the form of recommendations verifying that the person hired for the job will be qualified. It is this intoxication with information that lies at the foundation of the recommendation system.

This situation requires an intervention. Because the workplace has developed such an unhealthy use of recommendations, it is now suffering from *Recommendation Intoxication,* a habit that has become an ingrained tradition. Moreover, the workplace needs to go *to recommendation rehabilitation* where it can face the truth about its dependency on this form of professional assessment.

And what is the truth?

The truth is that recommendations are so subjective that they are meaningless. Further, this assessment system harbors elements that block the success of the workplace.

We pretend that recommendations have *everything* to do with work skills and nothing to do with murder, mayhem, power, sex, and deceit. Not so. The stories in this book are real-life situations that show this reality and the high price we pay for relying on this system.

In the following chapters, one word—recommendation—will be used to refer to both written and spoken recommendations, references, and referrals.

- A *letter of recommendation* is a document typically written by a former employer, supervisor, or teacher that endorses a person as a suitable job or academic candidate.
- A *reference* is a written or spoken statement, typically made by a former employer, supervisor, or teacher, that recommends a person as a suitable job or academic candidate.
- A *referral* is a written or spoken statement, typically made by former clients of a person, that recommends a person as a suitable business or service provider.
- *The recommendation system* is "a form of information that intoxicates and thwarts the success of the workplace." (Author)

Chapter Two

Recommendation Intoxication and the 2007 Recession

The lives of all people, from CEO to recent college grad, were altered by the economic recession that began in 2007. When the markets collapsed, it was clear that the world was paying an astronomical price for a series of extremely poor decisions. Even experts who understood the complexities of housing markets, hedge funds, credit default swaps, and Bernard Madoff-style ponzi schemes scrambled to explain how the economy deteriorated in such a drastic manner.

Journalists and commentators from Katie Couric, to Tavis Smiley, to Rush Limbaugh, sought to shed light on the problem by interviewing economists, politicians, and financial experts. But Katie, Tavis, and Rush did not ask two important questions:

1) What role did *recommendations* play in the collapse of the economy?

2) What will the continued use of the recommendation system cost the workplace?

These questions are critical because:

- Economic failure is caused by faulty business cultures and procedures. The recommendation system is an entrenched part of a culture that encourages the growth of unsound, unethical, and fraudulent business practices.
- The recommendation system is a time-honored tradition allegedly used to identify honorable and productive employees as well as honorable and productive business prospects. But the tradition has failed, costing us big bucks.
- A closer look reveals that the financial potential of people who do not understand the *true* power of *recommendations* is put at the mercy of those who know how to manipulate the system.
- The work and academic worlds must have accurate assessment to identify the best talent, not a recommendation system that is influenced by marketing strategies.

- The national unemployment rate reached a whopping 9.7 percent with 14 million out of work during the recession that began in 2007, and experts predict the workplace will continue to exhibit the impact of the economic upset for years to come. This job loss, paired with the trend toward downsizing and outsourcing, means that more Americans are competing for fewer jobs. For this reason, an accurate assessment of skills is vital to the success of the workplace.[3]
- Employers must promote and keep good workers to survive. The current recommendation system allows middle-manager gatekeepers to thwart this goal.
- Business decisions have huge financial impact. Business decisions that are based on recommendations jeopardize our financial futures.

Chapter Three

When Recommendation Intoxication Seduces You Into Making Costly Mistakes

Consider the proverb: "A good face is a letter of recommendation."

Now consider the revealing spin the following people— Dr. Ray Mettetal, financier Bernard Madoff, literary assistant C.W. Pattri, and commodities futures trader Thomas Farrell—would apply to this proverb. Knowing the stories of these people and their probable perspectives on *recommendations* explains in part how the economy collapsed.

Ray Mettetal, the Vanderbilt Hospital doctor, probably would add this twist to the proverb: A good face is essential to my career and worth *extreme measures.*

Adding to this idea, Bernard Madoff, whose pyramid scheme swindled some $50 billion from his clients, likely would say: The *appearance* of a good face is a letter of recommendation, *and to my benefit, people tend not to look beyond appearances.*

And on this point Madoff would be right. The New York financier and founder of Bernard L. Madoff Investment Securities LLC made headline news when authorities uncovered his long-running ponzi scheme. A ponzi scheme is a fraudulent investment tactic that leads investors to believe that their money will be invested and that they will receive unusually high profits with unusually low risk. In fact, the money is never invested, and investors are paid from their own funds until the money runs out and the scheme collapses. The ponzi scheme is named after Charles Ponzi, the infamous Italian swindler who journeyed to America and, during the 1920s, pocketed millions of dollars by luring people into his fake investment scheme.

Many well-established businesses, nonprofits, banks, and individuals trusted their money to Madoff Investment Securities. The long victim list included banks and investment companies, nonprofits (such as director Steven Spielberg's Wunderkinder Foundation), and individuals ranging from private citizens to celebrities. For example, actress Zsa Zsa Gabor reportedly lost some $10 million to Madoff's scam.[4]

Madoff's victims had resources to seek information that would have shed light on Madoff's fraudulent business practices. But *all* were beguiled, and then swindled, by the unscrupulous financier. As reported in a deluge of news stories, Madoff accomplished his scheme in part by the use of word-of-mouth referrals. These referrals were generated through Madoff's professional contacts on Wall Street and by his social contacts at the Palm Beach, Florida, country club where he was known as a generous philanthropist.

To their detriment, Madoff's victims did not look beyond their country club friends and Wall Street colleagues to discover information that would have protected them from Madoff's duplicity. Instead they relied on word-of-mouth recommendations, which allowed Madoff to capitalize on a common investment scam tactic known as "social consensus." Fraudsters such as Madoff use the social consensus tactic to lead people to believe that other people they know and trust have already invested, so the investment is sound.[5] This mistake cost them millions.

But the Madoff scandal not only shows the pitfalls of trusting a *good face*, it also is a starting point for recognizing that the recommendation system is an integral part of workplace practices that contributed to the collapse of the economy.

How so?

Consider the words of economist Nouriel Roubini who wrote:

"Americans lived in a 'Made-off' and Ponzi bubble economy for a decade or even longer. Madoff is the mirror of the American economy and of its over-leveraged agents: a house of cards of leverage over leverage by households, financial firms and corporations that has now collapsed in a heap."[6]

In other words, American corporations, financial firms, government, and households have adopted a Madoff-style approach to business, attempting to amass wealth with no foundation and no questions asked. The recommendation system supports a similar unquestioning approach to business. In the wake of the recession, it is critical that the workplace examine the reasoning behind all practices and make an appropriate cultural shift or suffer the dismal consequences.

Many people were surprised and then horrified by the depths of Madoff's deception. But looking at history, people have been using a *good face* and the recommendation system to gain entry to other people's money for centuries.

But why does this duplicity continue to be successful?

Reporters hark back to economist J.K. Galbraith's idea that such schemes continue to succeed because people are suckers for sharp-dressed bankers. Galbraith illuminated this reality in 1960 when he said people get swindled because they are inclined to believe that a *good face* means that they are dealing with a person of integrity.[7]

For example, consider the story of literary assistant C.W. Pattri. Pattri, aware of this tendency in people, also relied on a *good face* and recommendations to pull off a deceitful forgery scam. However, unlike Madoff, Pattri avoided billion-dollar swindles. He preferred nickel and diming employers into the poor house.

Pattri gained notoriety when an 1879 *New York Times* article described how he obtained employment with a prominent physician named Dr. Fowler, using a letter of recommendation. Pattri then capitalized on the trust relationship established by the letter to pull off a forgery and swindle money from the doctor.

Pattri weaseled his way into the doctor's life by claiming to be a literary assistant and translator. He appeared to be just the sort of employee the doctor was looking for to help prepare a medical manuscript for publication.

The *New York Times* article described Pattri's *good face*—"a German…about 35 years, of a pleasing dress and cool manners." Such a man, on the surface, appeared to be honest and capable of doing the work the doctor required. Further, Pattri paired his *good face* with both a *letter of recommendation* and a spoken reference from the American Public Health Association that described Pattri as "a gentleman and a scholar." On this basis, the doctor hired Pattri. But soon the doctor discovered that Pattri's skills did not match the qualifications described by the association, so the doctor fired Pattri.

Even so, the doctor wrote Pattri a positive letter recommending him as a good employee and an honest person.

Shortly thereafter, the doctor learned a hard lesson about trust in a *good face* and an uninvestigated recommendation when Pattri re-entered the scene to ask for money. Pattri paired his request with another letter from the American Public Health Association endorsing his need for temporary financial assistance.

Pattri's *good face* and the good letter from the association were persuasive. Without further inquiry, the doctor loaned Pattri a total of $60 in $5 to $25 increments—approximately $1,390 in today's currency.[8]

Unfortunately for the doctor, Pattri had forged the money request letter. Further, investigators discovered that Pattri was, in fact, a convict who had been released from New York's Sing Sing Prison only a few days before the association originally recommended him to the doctor. Although he realized the power of recommendations too late to help himself, the doctor sought to retrieve the letter he wrote for Pattri, presumably to protect his own integrity as a recommender.[9]

Just as Pattri benefited from a benevolent but gullible recommender, so too did commodities futures trader Thomas Farrell. His likely take on the proverb would be: *When your good face has a smudge of dirt on it, a letter of recommendation cleans it right up.*

Farrell's story began in August 1993, when he was hired by the German company FESAG Financial Engineering Services to trade German securities futures. Farrell's job involved arranging futures contracts, which are agreements to buy or sell a commodity, currency, or financial instrument, at a specific price on a specific future date. Trading in futures is a high-risk endeavor where small sums of money are invested in return for big payoffs or significant savings at a future date. However, because of the nature of the market, the possibility of a large return is paired with the risk of a large loss.[10]

Allegedly FESAG hired Farrell in part because of a letter of recommendation written by Patrick Arbor, the chairman of the Chicago Board of Trade. Arbor's letter affirmed Farrell's good qualities saying:

"I have known Tom Farrell personally for over 13 years. He was an active and full member of the Chicago Board of

Trade. Tom has always proven to be an intelligent, industrious, and innovative young man."

When FESAG hired Farrell, Farrell was directed to have no more than ten futures contracts open. An open futures contract is one that has not been liquidated or sold. But in September 1993, over a two-hour period while Farrell was working without supervision, Farrell violated this directive and maneuvered himself and FESAG into a situation where more than 5,900 futures contracts were open. According to FESAG, Farrell's actions caused FESAG to lose $5 million.[11]

Upon further investigation, FESAG discovered that the Chicago Futures Trading Commission had barred Farrell from trading on any futures exchange for a period of two years. Moreover, the commission had revoked Farrell's floor broker registration permanently. These actions were taken just one month before FESAG hired Farrell. FESAG took Farrell's recommender, Arbor, to court and lost. The court ruled that Arbor was not required to disclose this information about Farrell to FESAG. So in the end, FESAG learned a costly lesson about taking recommendations at face value.

Mettetal, Madoff, Pattri, Fowler, and Farrell remind us in stark detail that people have a deeply imbedded *belief* in the tradition of *recommendations.* So powerful is this belief that people go to extreme measures in pursuit of recommendations. So powerful is this belief that it seduces competent people charged with making business decisions to be deceived by a *good face*. And if the *good face* is smudged, a recommendation can cure this flaw to the detriment of those who do not take a closer look.

Chapter Four

Making a Deal with the Devil

In 2009, Oprah Winfrey brought much needed national attention to the long ignored but often devastating problem of school yard bullying following the tragic death of an eleven-year-old child who committed suicide after being bullied by his classmates. Oprah focused on the growing epidemic of bullying that has led to the victimization and deaths of children attending the nation's schools. But bullying is not exclusive to the playground. And, as any good parent knows, undesirable behaviors that are not addressed in children, such as bullying in the school yard, lead to children who grow up to be bullies. Consider what happens when the playground bully grows up and becomes a workplace manager who uses his or her power to control recommendations:

"Help. My boss is a bully. He controls through anger. He has a revolving door of admins, and the only reason I've lasted so long is because I know to keep my mouth shut. Another woman here can say the same about him (and has, to me). All the others have left, some after mere months…Telling him he has anger issues is

*a non-starter, he would only retaliate (even if under the radar—
i.e. why is that big bad project in my lap now? Because he is
mad...)."*[12]

Most employees can recall a story about a bullying boss, or they know someone who has had a similar experience. This fact paired with the world of high-fashion magazines equals the storyline of the popular movie *The Devil Wears Prada*. This movie tells the story of an editorial assistant who suffers through working for a devilish boss who uses bully tactics to manipulate employees. The film reportedly grossed some $300 million in revenue and made the top twenty list of hit movies released in 2006—evidence that people identify with the bullying boss situation.

At the movie's turning point, the editorial assistant walks off the job realizing that she can do better than her bullying boss situation. After leaving the magazine job, the heroine obtains a fantastic job as a news reporter, comes through her experience looking more beautiful than ever, and gets the guy of her dreams to boot. But the movie's seemingly happy ending left out two important details—the part where the editorial assistant must ask her former boss for a recommendation and the part where the hiring professional at the financially faltering magazine must go through the costly process of replacing the editorial assistant. This next chapter fills in the sobering details that the movie left out and reveals the real-world costs of bullying bosses.

Many people view devilish bosses as annoyances that employees must tolerate. But the truth is that these little devils are a big problem because they siphon money from businesses at an alarming rate.

How?

Bullying bosses tie their employees to them with the recommendation system. And this unreliable system gives bullying bosses the power and permission to drain businesses financially.

An astounding 54 million Americans report being bullied in the workplace, according to a 2007 Workplace Bullying Institute survey. Moreover, 72 percent of workplace bullies are bosses. Amazingly, 62 percent of employers ignore the problem.[13] But ignoring office bullying costs businesses big bucks, because a "bully culture" results in a revolving door of employees.

According to studies on business culture, 80 percent of employee turnover is caused by devilish boss situations.[14] People leave bosses, not jobs. Experts estimate that such turnover costs companies a staggering two to five times the departing employee's annual salary. And often companies do not realize that it costs more to hire new people than to keep current employees.[15]

Take the example of a bullying boss who receives praise for making budget cuts that save the company $60,000. Big savings? Not really. That savings is lost when the same boss bullies an employee who makes $60,000 a year out of his or her job. The turnover costs associated with replacing that employee likely will be $120,000 to $300,000. In a revolving-door scenario, bullying-related turnover results in the loss of hundreds of thousands of dollars a year.

Moreover, when *not* blocked by bully tactics, capable employees would naturally advance to positions where they increase the company's profits or move to other companies where they would excel. But effective bullies use recommendations to thwart this movement within the organization and throughout the marketplace. For example, a bully may use recommendation techniques—ranging from the subtle to the blatant—to block this movement. Subtle recommendation tactics include using a negative tone of voice, hesitation, or disparaging remarks sandwiched among compliments.

For example, an office manager may say that the candidate is well-spoken, is a nice person, but lacks attention to detail. According to the Workplace Bullying Institute, other common tactics include falsely accusing the target of making errors, criticizing the target continuously, having a different expectation for the target's performance, or facilitating damaging gossip about the target.[16]

This next story illustrates the blatant use of gossip within the recommendation system to block an employee from moving to another position.

Office manager Kellie Bowers said in a 2004 interview that she "couldn't believe her ears" when a reference told her the job candidate Bowers was investigating could be recommended only for employment in "a brothel or a strip joint."[17] In this case, Bowers' client reportedly sued the former employer for defamation, asking for $85 million in damages. Not only did the former employer have to field the cost of replacing the former employee, but the employer also had to face litigation costs.[18]

The profit-killing power wielded by bullying bosses is strengthened by the fact that, too often, one person—the boss or supervisor—is the sole source of recommendations for employees. Unfortunately, some prospective employers who receive disparaging information from such bosses take damaging remarks at face value and do not hire or promote otherwise good workers.

While garden variety office bullying is not illegal, one form—sexual harassment—*is* illegal. The Equal Employment Opportunity Commission received 12,696 sexual harassment claims in fiscal year 2009.[19] And this figure may be misleading because many harassed employees simply leave their jobs. Meanwhile, employers eat the hefty costs of this turnover. Further, problems occur for businesses and employees when the harasser is in charge of recommendations.

For example, the 1991 Senate investigation of Clarence Thomas, then a Supreme Court Justice nominee, raised the recommendation issue. The investigation involved Thomas' conduct toward his former employee, attorney Anita Hill. Hill alleged that Thomas sexually harassed her during the time she worked for him. Thomas denied the allegations.

The recommendation link here?

At one point in her career, Hill applied for a teaching position with the Oral Roberts University, a premier Christian institution in Tulsa, Oklahoma. She asked Thomas for a recommendation, which he provided. Subsequently she was hired by the university, so it is likely that the recommendation Thomas provided for Hill contained a positive assessment of Hill's work and professionalism. However, after Hill testified before the Senate about her work experiences with Thomas at the Equal Employment Opportunity Commission, Thomas' assessment of Hill appeared to change. In his memoir written in 2007, Thomas referred to Hill as a "mediocre" employee who was "touchy and apt to overreact" and who had expressed no religious sentiment. He also wrote in his biography, *My Grandfather's Son*, that the only reason Hill had obtained a job in the Reagan administration was that he had "given" it to her, not because she was qualified. One can imagine, based on these comments, what the text of Thomas' letter to the Oral Roberts University search committee *should* have looked like:

◆ ◆ ◆

Dear Search Committee:

I am pleased to recommend Anita Hill, a mediocre, over reactive, and ungodly woman, who is employed solely on the basis of my extreme generosity, and not because she is qualified for a teaching position at your prestigious school…

◆ ◆ ◆

Oral Roberts University likely would not have hired Hill had Thomas sent a lackluster recommendation. So which assessment—the letter sent to Oral Roberts University or the assessment in Thomas' autobiography—is accurate? Either way, a Thomas-type recommender is incapable of producing a reliable assessment.

Why?

Because an accurate assessment would not change after an employee challenges the use of power within supervisor-employee interactions.

Today Hill is a well-regarded law and policy professor at Brandeis University—a stellar accomplishment in its own right. But had Hill not been tied to Thomas through the recommendation system, what trajectory might her career have taken? In fact, in October 2010, two decades after the senate investigation, Hill received a phone message from Thomas' second wife, Ginni Thomas, asking Hill to issue a public apology for accusing him of sexual harassment. The phone message received great attention and was widely publicized.

For example, comedian Whoopie Goldberg read the phone message on the national television show *The View*. Hill reportedly said she did not intend to apologize because she had nothing to apologize for. Clearly this situation shows that negative recommendations have a long shelf life.

For many, it may not be clear who the villain was in the Hill-Thomas debate, but what should be clear is that the situation illustrates a defect in the recommendation tradition.

When bullying supervisors, from the office gossip to the sexual harasser, are given unchecked power through the recommendation system, both employees and employers pay a high price. The statistics—54 million bullied American workers and 12,696 sexual harassment claims filed with the Equal Employment Opportunity Commission—reveal the sobering reality that the misuse of power continues to plague the workplace. American businesses that ignore this reality and that continue to allow middle-managers to wield recommendation power— draining businesses financially—are suffering from recommendation intoxication and, moreover, are making a deal with the devil. But even so, employers doggedly continue to ignore the impact of recommendations provided by bullying bosses.

Can we afford to leave the assessment of our professional and economic potential in the hands of bullying bosses?

Hardly. Devilish bullying tactics may be entertaining in a movie, but in the real world, such bosses drain talent out of the workplace.

Chapter Five

The 50 Percent Problem

When it comes to recommendation use, about 50 percent of employers have the wrong idea. And what about the remaining 50 percent of employers? They also have the wrong idea.

What exactly does this mean?

It means that about half of American employers do *not* provide recommendations. The other half *do* provide recommendations. Employers in both camps have adopted their approach to recommendations based on problems they have encountered with the system. However, both groups are focusing on the *wrong* problem, and that's a *big* problem indeed.

The Problem According to the 50 Percent of Employers Who Do Not Provide Recommendations

Some fifty percent of employers have a "no recommendations" policy. Such employers believe that providing recommendations exposes them to lawsuits. This fear arguably has some basis in reality. Once upon a time, in the pre-1980s workplace, employers commonly provided recommendations. When prospective employers called former employers to dish the dirt about job applicants, communication flowed freely. But then along came the turbulent 1980s, a decade when employers became nervous about providing employer-endorsed recommendations.

Why?

Because during this time, defamation lawsuits began to surface, causing employers to feel vulnerable to litigation costs. Clutching their bank accounts, employers ran to their lawyers seeking a "fix" to keep from being sued.

And how did the lawyers respond?

They counseled employers to stop providing employer-endorsed recommendations or to limit information to name, title, and dates of employment. And employers followed this advice.

Problem solved?

Not really.

The 1980s gave way to the 1990s and the trend of recommendation-related problems for employers continued.

The year was 1997, and the California Supreme Court had just ruled that employers could be liable for providing *positive* recommendations that misrepresent employees' suitability for future employment. The court case involved a thirteen-year-old student who alleged that she had been molested by her school principal, Robert Gadams. The student sued Gadams' former employer (another school) and won because Gadams' former employer had received similar complaints about him but failed to disclose this information in the recommendation. In fact, the employer's recommendation *praised* Gadams' professional skills and recommended him for the job of school principal without reservation.[20]

But the story does not end there. In the aftermath of this case and others, employers became increasingly nervous. They viewed this case as another avenue in a growing list of ways that they could be sued for providing information in recommendations. In fact, during the 1990s, some employers were sued for providing not only *positive* recommendations, but for providing *negative* and *neutral* recommendations as well. The *negative* reference case that inspired employers to zip their lips when it came to recommendations involved Shell Oil Company.

In 1991, Shell terminated the employment of sales representative Charles Robinson. Robinson believed he was fired because of his race, and he filed a charge with the Equal Employment Opportunity Commission to investigate Shell's actions. While the charge was being investigated, Robinson applied for a job with another company. The reference check for this job revealed that Shell had given Robinson a negative recommendation. Robinson claimed that the negative recommendation was given in retaliation for the discrimination charges he filed against Shell. When the case went before the U.S. Supreme Court, the court held that the protection against retaliation provided by Title VII of the Civil Rights Act of 1964 covered both current and former employees, thereby exposing employers to more money-grabbing litigation from current employees as well as former employees such as Robinson.[21]

To make matters worse, these already nervous employers were being exposed to litigation for giving *neutral* recommendations as well. The story of Paul Caulden and the five people Caulden shot in the workplace illustrates the *neutral* recommendation problem.

When Caulden was hired by the Allstate Insurance Company, he began the job on extremely odd footing in terms of his behavior. For example, Caulden declined to have his photograph taken, claiming that his likeness could not be recorded on film. Caulden also told people he was from another planet. And as if that were not enough to alert his employers that something was amiss, Caulden kept a list of coworkers' names next to which he had written the word "blood." Finally, in 1993, after nine months of employment with Allstate, Caulden was fired after a gun was found in his briefcase.

Reportedly Allstate, at that time, had a *no recommendations* policy. But in Caulden's case, Allstate drafted a *neutral* letter saying that he had resigned voluntarily when his position was eliminated because of company restructuring.

After leaving Allstate, Caulden took this *neutral* recommendation to Fireman's Fund and was hired, in part, because of the recommendation. However, Fireman's Fund later fired Caulden. After Caulden was fired, he returned to the Fireman's Fund employee cafeteria located in Tampa, Florida, and shot five supervisors, resulting in three deaths. The families of the shooting victims sued Allstate for not revealing Caulden's odd behavior in the *neutral* recommendation. Allstate later settled the case.[22]

Recall that on the heels of exposure to defamation lawsuits in the 1980s, lawyers counseled employers to protect themselves by terminating the practice of providing employer-endorsed recommendations. This trend continued and became entrenched throughout the 1990s. Consequently today more than half of employers have a *no recommendations* policy. Under the *no recommendations* policy, employers provide only name, title, and dates of employment.[23]

But this tactic has resulted in unanticipated repercussions.

The problem?

Because half of employers no longer share information about job applicants, access to detailed information has been severely limited for *all* employers.[24]

Consequently many employers still require job applicants to provide recommendations whether they work for an employer who is willing to provide them or not. This trend raises the question—How do job applicants whose former employers do not provide recommendations produce the recommendations required by prospective employers? The answer is—they can't. What they *can* do is identify former supervisors willing to provide recommendations as private individuals rather than on behalf of the employer. And this is precisely what people seeking jobs do.

Prospective employers readily accept recommendations provided by job applicants' former supervisors. In fact, according to a recent Society for Human Resource Management survey, 66 percent of employers require applicants to provide references from *at least one previous* employer *or supervisor*, and 19 percent specifically require a reference from the applicant's *current* employer *or supervisor*.[25]

Employers seem to believe that this practice of seeking recommendations from former supervisors in this manner solves the problem. The thought process goes something like this:

We like our money, so we don't want to be sued and have to give up some of our money. If we stop providing employer-endorsed recommendations and promote the flow of recommendations from someone who is not acting on our behalf (supervisors acting as individuals), then, when the &*979! hits the fan, we will not be the party held responsible for comments in recommendations. We can still get information we need to hire good employees and stay out of the lawsuit fray. And if there's trouble, it's those unfortunate managers and former job applicants who have to duke it out...

The only problem with this approach—seeking recommendations from former supervisors acting as individuals—is that employers still get sued. Disgruntled employees still sue employers over the comments made in recommendations, even when the employer has a "no recommendations policy." Further, the practice of requiring recommendations from former supervisors acting as individuals encourages the troubling practice of supervisors and managers providing recommendations without training, knowledge of legal issues, or oversight. This practice keeps the unreliable recommendation system going, while making the unreliability of the system more potent by putting it into the hands of supervisors who, be they well intentioned or not, are incapable of reliable assessment.

The Problem According to the 50 Percent of Employers Who Do Provide Recommendations

The other 50 percent of employers *do* provide some form of employer-endorsed recommendation. The employers who *do* provide recommendations believe that there is *no problem* with the recommendation system, or, if there is a problem, it is only a *small* problem that can be fixed by using methods they believe are more reliable, such as the use of standardized recommendation forms or performance evaluations.

A standardized recommendation form is a document that allows employers to rate employees using multiple choice and number ranges instead of "free form" comments. A performance evaluation is typically an annual assessment of an employee's work, which the employee and supervisor review together. The performance evaluation is then reviewed further by a human resources department.

Both types of assessment leave no room for the recommender's comments, but neither solves the unreliability problem. A recommender can insert an opinion into a standardized form by simply selecting the choice that reflects his or her bias. On a recommender's good day an employee may be rated "excellent" and on a bad day that same recommender may rate that same employee as "insufficient." Further, performance evaluations are often linked to benefits, such as competitive bonuses, and employees may be informally counseled by supervisors to rate themselves higher or lower so that bonuses can be distributed in a particular manner.

The Right Problem? Recommendation Intoxication

Both camps of employers (those who *do* provide recommendations and those who *do not* provide recommendations) have described the problem with the recommendation tradition in different ways, but both have misidentified the problem. The most useful description of the problem is that the recommendation system is an intoxicating but unreliable habit that should be abandoned.

But if describing the recommendation problem is that simple, why does the workplace continue to mischaracterize the problem?

Because the hardwiring of the human brain has trumped our ability to make well-reasoned decisions. Recommendations give workplace participants a buzz—we feel good and more in control when we use information obtained through recommendations, so there is little motivation to question the practice. But the workplace is actually *not* in control when using recommendations to make decisions, and this approach to business comes at a cost.

The Costs of Recommendation Intoxication

Cost for Employers
As we have seen in previous stories, reliance on unreliable information when making business decisions is

financial suicide. Just as the *good face* or the *devilish boss* generate unreliable information that derails good decisions, so do recommendations. And when it comes to recommendations provided by supervisors on an informal basis, the danger is that the reliability of such assessments generally goes unchallenged. This lack of oversight fails to reveal a variety of flaws in both the recommender and the person being recommended. But flaws exist. If businesses are serious about maximizing profits in a tough market by hiring and retaining the best people, then surrendering the recommendation power to middle managers, whose assessments are not foolproof, derails that goal.

Cost for Employees

The professional goals of employees are also derailed by the non-employer-endorsed recommendation approach. When job applicants give prospective employers the names of recommenders who are willing to provide informal rather than employer-endorsed recommendations, such applicants are participating in an unreliable information exchange that will shape their professional futures. Further, employees may never know the good, the bad, and the ugly of the informal comments made about their professional skills and character. In an economy where competition for jobs is fierce, employees should never lose sight of the high cost of participation in this system. Even employees who believe they have received only sterling non-employer-endorsed recommendations should not be lulled into a false sense of security. Each encounter employees have with the rec-ommendation system (employer-endorsed or informal)—through job changes or potential promotions—is fraught with the pitfalls of this unreliable system.

Chapter Six:

Workplace Violence and Recommendation Intoxication

❖❖❖

Dear University of Alabama:

Amy Bishop is a highly skilled biology researcher who has an impressive Ivy League pedigree. She also happens to be disturbingly violent. She once punched out a woman at an International House of Pancakes restaurant because the woman had taken the last children's booster seat. And no less disturbing, she reportedly was responsible for the death of her brother when she was 18 years old. Past patterns often repeat themselves, so you probably can expect more of the same should you hire this candidate. However, I recommend her for this position without reservation...

Signed,

The Recommender for Biology Professor Amy Bishop

❖❖❖

It is not likely that the University of Alabama search committee received such a letter before hiring Amy Bishop, the disgruntled biology professor who shot and killed three colleagues during a faculty meeting on February 12, 2009.

Why?

Because a recounting of violent behavior is exactly the type of detail that employers balk at disclosing through the recommendation system.

Now recall for a moment Paul Caulden, the disgruntled insurance worker who shot five people on the job, and Robert Gadams, the alleged pedophile principal. Such stories are not just about employers and their money—rather they are about real people getting *really* hurt. On a daily basis, news outlets report occurrences of murder, mayhem, and victimization in the workplace and in schools. Such harrowing stories, played and re-played in the news, make workplace violence appear to be rampant and on the rise. But in reality, the number of workplace homicides has dropped more than 50 percent since 1994.[26]

However, this fact is no consolation for victims of workplace violence and their families or for employers who are charged with the safety of their workers. Moreover, the clean-up cost of workplace violence is high for employers. Such costs may include: litigation, therapy for victims and employees, turnover, and damage to the employer's reputation. For these reasons, employers have searched for ways to protect themselves so they can screen potentially dangerous applicants and prevent violence before it occurs.

Their solution?

Create laws that encourage employers to share information about violent workers through the recommendation system.

How so?

During the 1990s, states started enacting "reference immunity" (also referred to as "employer immunity") statutes, designed to protect employers willing to share information during reference checks about violent employees. Currently more than half of the states in the United States have "reference immunity" statutes. Such statutes do not require employers to disclose information, but do provide a level of protection for employers who share information during reference checks.

The nature and level of protection provided to employers varies from state to state. However, the general policy reason for such legislation has been to encourage the free flow of information among employers to prevent incompetence and violence from entering the workplace. State statutes vary with respect to the type of information that employers may disclose. Some state statutes give employers protection for disclosing information ranging from general competence to violence.

On the whole, "reference immunity" statutes have been both applauded and criticized for a variety of reasons. But the major criticism is that the statutes have failed to change employer behavior. With or without immunity statutes, employers are running scared, unwilling to share information beyond name, title, and dates of employment.

So what is wrong with the reference immunity solution?

First, employers still remain unprotected from lawsuits, so they are not willing to have an open information exchange.

Second, these statutes are based on the premise that the recommendation system actually works. But the news accounts of Bishop, Caulden, and Gadams show that violent behavior typically brews beneath the surface for years, noticed but not disclosed by employers through the recommendation system. This being the case, the recommendation system fails to protect workers from office violence.

Moreover, garden variety incompetence on the job and violence in the workplace are two different animals. The activity of "Employee Joe" being late to work on a daily basis is different in nature and degree from the activity of "Employee Joe" being a pedophile or a murderer. When it comes to safety as a goal, state statutes that rely on the recommendation system to communicate the propensity for violence and that combine employee competence issues with violence issues are at best ineffectual and at worst irresponsible.

So how can employers prevent violence in the workplace?

Discarding the recommendation system does not mean that employers should not take responsibility for disclosing violent behavior. Employers should be required by law to document violence and threats and disclose this information during the employment verification process. Clearly, disclosure of name, title, dates of employment, and any violent behavior does not have to be, and moreover should not be, combined with the unreliable recommendation system. Instead, keen attention should be given to areas where steps can be taken toward meaningful solutions. For example, employers should have the resources to conduct thorough criminal background checks, but currently many do not.

Why?

Although criminal background information is public record, the main sources for this information are databases owned by private companies. Such companies purchase the information from states and counties, but unfortunately, these databases do not have complete information. Although the Federal Bureau of Investigation has access to a national crime database, the same information is not available to the public. Therefore, employers do not have access to a national database that provides a record of *all* criminal convictions. To do a thorough background check, employers would have to visit each county and state court in person and search paper files—an insurmountable obstacle to getting accurate information.

Remedying this problem would be one concrete step toward providing real solutions to workplace violence. Continuing to cobble together a solution using the flawed recommendation system is a recipe for inaction (on the part of employers) and more Amy Bishop-style violence in the workplace.

Chapter Seven

The Un-Vetted Recommender

When a break from real-world problems, such as the economy, is needed, we often escape to the world of celebrity gossip. From the marital bliss of actors Tom Cruise and Katie Holmes to the international family of Angelina Jolie, the celebrity industry's success depends entirely on our willingness to engage in the flawed thinking that the lives and contributions of the rich and famous are more valid than our own contributions. But when celebrity and recommendation intoxication collide, a closer look is needed. Recommendations weakened with celebrity trivia and other off-point and inappropriate details are more than amusing distractions. Such recommendations provide further evidence that the recommendation system is flawed and should be abandoned.

Case in point:

Angelina Jolie—acclaimed actress, children's advocate, and humanitarian ambassador—is a citizen of Cambodia. True or false?

True. Jolie is, in fact, an honorary citizen of Cambodia. The honor was bestowed on her in 2005 by King Norodom Sihamoni based on her humanitarian work. But this bit of celebrity trivia had absolutely nothing to do with the work and skills of one Cambodian student who applied for admission to a prominent U.S. business school. The applicant's apparently star-struck recommender decided it would lend the applicant cache to include this unrelated detail in a letter supporting the applicant's admission to the school.[27] In fact, such off-point comments are not uncommon. Admissions officers and hiring professionals across the nation often receive recommendations that include a variety of irrelevant, attention-getting details.

For example, some recommenders promote their own pedigrees instead of the candidate's skills. In one instance, a recommender, evidently a self-absorbed family historian, addressed the applicant's skills but also included information about the recommender's Pilgrim ancestors who had sailed to the United States on the *Mayflower*.[28] Studies show that when recommenders provide such irrelevant information or focus on their own pedigrees and qualifications instead of on the applicant, it gives the impression that the recommenders have nothing meaningful to report about the applicant.[29]

Along with celebrity trivia and self-promotion, admissions officers and hiring professionals must navigate their way through a minefield of obstacles to reliable assessment. These obstacles often include details beyond the applicant's control, such as the recommender's poor grammar. If the letter reader is a stickler for grammar, the recommender's letter might be unfairly dismissed.

Such situations have led to the creation of industries that profit from guiding people through the recommendation process. These guides offer tips on providing recommendations that market applicants in a competitive manner. Many guides also discuss how recommenders can avoid liability. In fact, a 2009 search of Google for the terms "letter of recommendation and/or references" produced 1,380,000 search results, clear evidence that recommendations are high on the nation's anxiety scale.[30]

This abundance of information reveals that the recommendation tradition is deeply entrenched in the academic and workplace cultures.

While this massive self-help industry may assuage our anxiety, it does not define or solve one central problem with the recommendation system—vetting the recommenders.

Vetting is the practice of investigating the history, skills, and character of applicants. The techniques used and the extent of inquiry during the vetting process vary among industries. Popularly, vetting is an approach used to assess the suitability of political candidates. In this context, political operatives leave no stone unturned in an effort to find negative information about opposing candidates.

Technologies such as Twitter have expanded the practice of vetting. Twitter is a popular social networking site that allows people to socialize online by sending "tweets" to each other that provide up-to-the-minute details of daily activities. According to news reports, Twitter recently announced it would vet the twitter accounts allegedly created by politicians, government entities, and celebrities, in order to verify that the accounts are authentic. For example, fans of the tweets sent from the White House and from celebrities such as actor Ashton Kutcher now can take solace in knowing that the tweets received from President Obama and Kutcher have been vetted and are the real deal.

According to a variety of sources, the term "vet" originally was used in the horse racing industry. Historically, horse owners called in a veterinarian to examine a horse and certify its soundness for racing. In the employment arena, hiring professionals are much like these veterinarians, political operatives, and Twitter account verifiers, except their job is to examine applicants' soundness for employment.

But how sound are the recommenders?

While 96 percent of employers reportedly attempt to investigate the background of applicants, few, if any, employers vet the *recommenders*.[31] This failure to investigate the suitability of recommenders is a fatal weakness of the recommendation system. Clearly, in order for an assessment tool to be reliable, people must be able to measure the accuracy of the tool. But the developing picture of the recommendation system shows that many admissions officers and hiring professionals may take recommendations at face value, making little or no effort to vet recommenders. Consequently, they have little information about the recommender's professionalism, ethics, or mental state. The un-vetted recommender hurts employers because employers need accurate assessments to elevate the hiring process from a guessing game to a profitable practice. Unfortunately, the developing picture of the un-vetted recommender reveals the depths of dysfunction in the recommendation system.

And interestingly, studies show that recommendations may actually reveal more about the *recommender* than the *person being recommended*.[32]

The following situations illustrate this phenomenon and reveal flaws in the recommendation system that highlight the critical need for employers to recognize and address the vetting problem:

The Perception Flaw

Perception is high on this list of flaws. What people perceive as positive or negative varies from person to person.

Consider the situation of poets Eileen Myles, the recommendation requester, and John Ashbery, the recommender. Ashbery, a colleague of Myles, wrote a letter of recommendation for her. Sometime later, Myles unexpectedly discovered the contents of the letter. She made public her concerns about Ashbery's comments within the pages of the *Chicago Review*. She wrote:

"I found out a few years back that for many years the recommendation from John Ashbery that I had been using opened with the language: 'Eileen Myles is a militant lesbian.' I sent it for jobs where I definitely knew people on the committee. Finally a total stranger at one of those institutions that maintain recommendations told me on the QT that I shouldn't use it. I managed to get my hands on it and I was stunned. That's when I felt totally outside

the poetry community, because I realized that no one protected me. Nobody thought it was politically offensive or destructive. They probably thought it was funny."[33]

Ashbery responded to Myles' concerns by writing a letter to the editor saying that he had "always liked Eileen and admired her poetry." Further, he said that his intention was to write a positive recommendation for her and believed his comments were non-offensive. To prove his intentions, Ashbery included his original letter, which read:

"Poet, militant lesbian, critical gadfly, and unsuccessful 1992 presidential candidate, Eileen Myles has been shaking up the downtown poetry scene for quite some time, including several years as the director of Saint Mark's Poetry Project. Her political activism and uncanny knack for making people feel uncomfortable and awake have sometimes obscured the fact of what a fine poet she is. Indeed, her poetry often works in diverging directions, chanting softly and beautifully the harsh if humorous realities that combine to make whatever life a poet can piece together today. I have observed her teaching, and noticed that her mere presence seems to electrify an eager group of students. She's always sharp, always there—a valuable asset to any teaching institution."[34]

The Myles-Ashbery situation shows how the perceptions of the recommender, applicant, and hiring professional varied. Clearly such variations impact the assessment of applicants.

We have just seen how the recommender's eccentricities or perceptions about appropriateness water down the value of recommendations. Add to this mix other flaws, including pharmaceuticals, gender bias, and the diseased culture of a "troubled" business and you have a volatile cocktail guaranteeing that suitable employees will be rejected and unsuitable employees will be hired. The following recommendation situations show how such flaws materialize in the workplace.

The Pharmaceutical Flaw

On a daily basis, workers head to the office with prescription pain killers, cigarettes, and Starbucks' vente soy cappuccinos in their hands—the workplace is a mood-altered environment, and this impacts recommendations.[35]

Janice (not her real name) worked for Dan (not his real name).[36] She enjoyed her work and believed that she generally had a good working relationship with Dan. However, Janice was aware that Dan was subject to mood swings triggered by prescription medications. Janice was also aware that employees avoided Dan when it came time to ask for recommendations.

Why?

Dan's mood dictated the type of recommendation he provided. On his good days, Dan perceived his employees as skilled and competent, but on his bad days, Dan perceived his employees as incompetent slackers.

The Gender Bias Flaw

Just as prescription drug use can distort recommendations, so can gender bias. Studies comparing recommendations for male and female applicants for faculty positions show that, generally, the personal lives of female applicants are mentioned six times more often than the personal lives of male applicants.[37]

Studies also show that letters for women focus on their training and teaching skills, while letters for men focus more on higher-value traits such as research, success, and professionalism.[38] Further, letters written for women focused on effort while letters for men focused on ability and included more specific descriptions of their research and accomplishments. Moreover, comments describing a close personal social contact with the applicant and comments about personal and health issues were included more often for women than for men.

Consider the following letter reportedly written for a female applicant for a position as a professor of pulmonary medicine:

"Sarah's personal life was in turmoil during the time I worked with her, and in view of the difficulties she was experiencing in that area, her performance was especially impressive. Her last years in my laboratory were impacted by serious health problems that have fortunately gone away—she had really debilitating problems with a herniated disk that apparently was a paraneplastic phenomenon that went away once an early carcinoma of the left ovary was identified and removed..."[39]

Other letters from the same study included examples of comments made about personal ties to female applicants that did not appear as often in letters written for men.

One recommender wrote:

"…I have known Sarah for approximately four years, becoming socially friendly with her and her husband…Sarah is quite close to my wife, and they frequently seek each other's company out…"[40]

Clearly this level of personal detail is borderline to wholly inappropriate and possibly damaging to female applicants.

The Race Bias Flaw

Searches of databases failed to reveal current studies published on race and recommendations. But a closely related topic—the impact of race bias on performance evaluations—points to the critical need for more research on possible detrimental effects of race bias within the recommendation system.

Performance evaluations are simply formalized internal recommendations. As such, it is likely that supervisors may base recommendations for future employment, in part, on employees' performance evaluations.

A 1990 performance evaluation study found that if you are a white woman and you have a black man as a supervisor you are indeed a lucky employee, because white female employees typically receive higher ratings on evaluations than white men or black women working for a black male supervisor. But if you are a black man and you have a white male or white female supervisor, you are not so fortunate, because studies of the workplace have shown that white supervisors rate the job performance of blacks "less favorably" than the performance of whites.[41]

If these studies are accurate, that would mean that there is a pecking order in the workplace when it comes to performance evaluations. But what about recommendations? Would the same pecking order exist under the recommendation system?

Current studies specifically designed to identify a "race-based pecking order" in the recommendation system could not be located at the time of this writing. However, one 1992 study suggests that the race of the recommender may contribute to the unreliability of the recommendation system. The study showed that black recommenders tend to be more lenient and positive in their comments regardless of the race of the person being recommended.[42]

So what can be gleaned from the fact that black male supervisors rate white men and black women lower than white women on performance evaluations but make more positive comments generally in recommendations regardless of the race of the person they are recommending? And what about non-white groups other than black people? How do other non-white groups fare in the recommendation system? Clearly race bias is part of the recommendation system, and this impacts the accuracy of assessment through recommendations.

The Troubled Business Flaw

One of the rare situations where employers show awareness of the *vetting the recommender* problem is the "troubled" business predicament. A "troubled" business is one that is incapable of providing recommendations for former employees because the business has contracted a communicable disease—a negative reputation.

The recent poster child for the "troubled" business is Bernard L. Madoff Investment Securities.

In June 2009, while Madoff was being sentenced to 150 years in prison for investment fraud, his former employees were left searching for jobs with the albatross of his investment company's negative reputation attached to their resumes. Employees who entertained the notion of asking their supervisors or Madoff himself for recommendations found this option closed to them.

When interviewed, hiring professionals varied in their opinions of applicants who had worked for troubled businesses such as Madoff Investments. Some hiring professionals reported that working for a bad company does not necessarily make an applicant a bad prospect. Others held the opinion that an applicant's positive attitude could put a positive spin on a negative situation. Still others believed that the applicant's closeness to the chain of wrongdoing would make the difference. And some said the company's reputation, without question, would be a mark against a job applicant in a tight market.[43]

But does the workplace have to experience the boiling point of a "troubled" company situation before employers recognize the un-vetted recommender problem?

Human beings are flawed, and their flaws show up in recommendations. Unfortunately, identifying and investigating such flawed information is not a priority for hiring professionals. But such a priority is critical if the recommendation system is to be continued. Businesses serious about improving their position in a tough economy must be aware of the un-vetted recommender problem and must commit to a sure course of action.

Imagine for a moment a workplace where all recommenders are vetted. Under such a scenario, the recommender's ability to make a reliable assessment itself would be under scrutiny. Investigating the recommender's background would mean the end of unfettered fate control by recommenders and the beginning of holding such gatekeepers accountable for the financial impact of their assessments—a sobering prospect for many recommenders.

Now imagine the impact on human resources staff if recommenders are vetted. Most human resources staff have neither the time nor the people power to investigate the backgrounds of recommenders. And ultimately, because all recommendations are suspect (no matter how many generations of recommenders are vetted), such a practice would not shed more light on a job candidate's suitability. In reality, vetting the recommenders would be as unreliable as the continued use of the current recommendation system.

The solution?

Choose sobriety over Recommendation Intoxication— discontinue the recommendation system.

Meanwhile, as the workplace ignores the vetting problem, some savvy employees, in a defensive move, are vetting the individuals they ask to be recommenders. In fact, a lucrative industry has been created to support this practice. The next chapter explores the cloak-and-dagger world of the people hired to vet recommenders. They are referred to by some as "job detectives."[44]

Chapter Eight

Enter the Job Detectives

Put an ear to the door of a typical office and likely you will hear the details of at least one office romance circulating through the rumor mill. Typically such gossip about events, real or imagined, stays in the rumor mill *unless you are a particular type of recommender*. Picture this scenario pulled from a current news story. An employer conducting a reference check on a job applicant calls the applicant's former manager. During the conversation, the manager says the applicant had an affair with another employee. Further, this couple had a baby together, which led to the male employee's divorce.[45]

This story provides one of many examples of how inappropriate information can be transmitted through the recommendation system.

The comments made by the manager in this story were discovered by a reference-checking firm that investigates references provided by former supervisors.

Called "job detectives" by some, this industry grew out of the weaknesses of the recommendation system. One such business, Documented Reference Check Inc., reports annual worldwide sales of $13,200,000.[46] Another company, Allison & Taylor Inc., states on its website that a full 50 percent of its calls to former employers "result in a bad reference."[47]

Reference-checking companies of this type reportedly may employ court reporters who, using the name of an affiliated firm to conceal their identities, call former supervisors and managers under the pretense of checking references. Their staff members reportedly record managers' comments and revealing nonverbal signs, such as disparaging voice tones or prolonged pauses before answering questions.[48]

Former employees use job detective information in two ways. They can dump the reference altogether or, if the comment is defamatory, they can, and do, sue, costing employers big bucks. People who have used such companies applaud their services:

"Prior to losing my job, I had no idea that your service even existed. In fact, the mere thought of verifying the quality of my own references never even crossed my mind. Thank goodness, a friend referred me to your firm. The research your company did uncovered one bad reference—the reason I wasn't receiving any job offers. This information allowed me to strategically avoid this individual and successfully land the next position I interviewed for." –J. Mcknight, V.P. Marketing.[49]

Recall the story of the manager who said a former employee could be recommended only for work in a brothel or a strip club. This manager's comments were discovered through a "job detective" reference-checking service. In this case, the former employee, armed with this information, sued her former employer for defamation and asked for $85 million in damages.[50]

For reasons illustrated by these stories, some reference-checking professionals advise employers against allowing middle managers to provide recommendations.[51] However, the same employers who protect themselves by following this advice may engage in the unwise practice of pressuring those applying for jobs to provide references from former managers.

This action by employers shifts the financial burden to job applicants. Under this system, the job applicants who want to ensure they're relaying favorable recommendations must pay "job detectives" to investigate the contents of recommendations provided by former managers. A typical fee in 2009 for a bad reference check was around $90.[52] However, this financial loss to employees is a gain in the long run because they are made aware of negative references.

Nevertheless, in this cloak-and-dagger game of catching bad recommendations, employers lose the most. Employers lose because employees can drop a bad recommendation and present a *good face* rather than an accurate picture of themselves. Employers also lose because they are exposed to litigation as employees increasingly turn to job detectives to protect the integrity of their professional reputations.

Discontinuing the recommendation system could diminish the need for job detectives. But the system must be changed for this to occur. In the meantime, employers beware—the "job detectives" may be listening to the comments made by middle managers about former employees, and it can cost you.

Chapter Nine

Feeding the Habit – Settlement Agreements and Severance Packages

Employers make a clever two-handed use of recommendations. On the one hand, more than half report that they do not provide recommendations for the purpose of assessing former employees. On the other hand, many employers (those who do not provide recommendations among them) are quick to offer recommendations in situations where employers think recommendations will help their position.

When does a recommendation help employers?

Recommendations help when offered as part of severance packages and settlement agreements designed to *keep things quiet* or to *stop the bleeding*. Employers *keep things quiet* by doling out recommendations to former employees who agree to keep their mouths shut, which allows employers to protect their reputations. Employers *stop the bleeding* by negotiating settlements that save money by cutting off costly litigation. Such settlements generally include a positive letter of recommendation. Recommendations for these purposes are unreliable and feed the workplace's recommendation intoxication habit.

Feeding the Habit (The Christian Coalition Story)

A scandal involving religion and large sums of money often generates the motivation to *keep things quiet*. Combine a religious scandal with the recommendation system and you have proof positive that recommendations are unreliable assessment tools.

Judy Liebert, the former chief financial officer for the Christian Coalition, experienced this reality in 1996, when she was fired after exposing the coalition's alleged involvement in making impermissible campaign contributions.[53] After firing Liebert, the coalition, a conservative evangelical advocacy group, offered her a severance package to head off litigation and safeguard the group's reputation. The coalition offered Liebert a positive recommendation, attorney fees, and $80,000 in severance pay. But there was a catch. To get the severance package, Liebert had to agree to keep her mouth shut regarding coalition activities.

Liebert, who reportedly started working for the coalition because of its Christian values, refused to sign the agreement, saying that she could not live with the prospect of having to conceal the truth about the coalition.[54] It is a workplace assumption that including recommendations as part of severances and settlements helps secure future employment and preserves the dignity of the terminated person. However, that does not appear to have happened in the Liebert situation. But equally as important as the preservation of dignity, the Liebert story illustrates how employers use the power of the recommendation system as both a carrot and a stick rather than as an assessment tool. That is, if you want future employment, don't talk.

A review of news stories on the topic reveals that these types of recommendations are produced through similar negotiations on a regular basis throughout the workplace.

In the News: The Bath Community Librarian

Bath, Maine, is a small New England city that has enjoyed an illustrious history. In 2009 it was named one of the "10 Great Places in America." And in 2005 it was named a "Distinctive Destination" by the National Trust for Historic Preservation.[55] But during the years between these awards, Bath became the subject of a great controversy that brewed in its public library. In September 2007, children's librarian Nyree Thomas, who worked for the Patten Free Library in Bath, was fired after she reportedly received an unsatisfactory review. However, aside from being a "Great Place in America" and a "Distinctive Destination," Bath had another characteristic not honored by these awards—good people who loved their librarians and valued their work. Indeed, after the Bath community discovered Thomas had been fired, it rallied to Thomas' defense. As a result, the library offered Thomas a positive recommendation, severance pay, and a public apology.[56] Whether Thomas was an unsatisfactory or an exemplary employee cannot be known from the contents of the recommendation she received from the library. The point to recognize is not Thomas' actual competence as a librarian, but the fact that she was given a good recommendation to prevent litigation and to repair the library's damaged relationship with the Bath community.

In the News: The Narcoleptic Hotel Employee

The Ritz Carlton Central Park, a luxury New York hotel, is known for celebrity sightings. Emmanual Okoro, who worked in the Ritz housekeeping department, likely experienced the thrill of seeing more than one famous face walking through the luxurious hotel. But more likely than that, he may have slept through a few sightings, not because of laziness, but because he suffered from narcolepsy, a neurological condition that causes a person to fall asleep without warning. A person with narcolepsy may fall asleep several times a day for periods of a few seconds to an hour or more.

The Ritz fired Okoro after a period of employment. Okoro reportedly believed he was fired because he had narcolepsy, and he promptly sued the Ritz for discrimination under the Americans With Disabilities Act. Ritz representatives requested that the lawsuit be dismissed because they had already offered Okoro a settlement and he had accepted its terms. According to Ritz representatives, the settlement included a positive letter of recommendation.

Incidentally, Okoro had no memory of signing the settlement agreement. But a more important detail to notice is that recommendations produced as a result of settlements are, by nature, suspect. Clearly the settlement and the recommendation provided to Okoro by way of the settlement was motivated by the hotel's goal to cut off litigation. Ironically, Okoro took the Ritz to court anyway.[57]

This is not to say that employers should be allowed to discriminate. And they certainly should not be permitted to cut off a good employee's future job prospects with poor recommendations. The point to recognize is that the recommendation system itself is unreliable, and recommendations resulting from settlements and severances feed the workplace's recommendation intoxication habit.

In the News: The Middle School Principal

In another example, a "neutral" letter of recommendation (listing name, position, and dates of employment) was included in a 2008 settlement agreement between the Douglas Unified School District and George Watkins, the principal of the Huber Middle School in Arizona. The Huber Middle School has an active honor society. In fact, the school's honor society raised $188 to support the school's activities through a juice-pop sale. Imagine the school district's chagrin when it discovered that Watkins reportedly had stolen the money from the sale. Watkins was fired, but he left with a neutral recommendation in hand.[58]

Most would agree that a tendency to take money from school children would impair an individual's ability to work as a principal—the school's number one role model. Even so, Watkins' alleged sticky-finger problem would not be discovered in the contents of the school's letter of recommendation.

In the News: The Public Radio General Manager

According to the recommendation written in 2008 for Patricia Wente, the general manager of the KWMU Public Radio station, the number of public radio listeners and membership increased significantly under Wente's management. The recommendation was written by the University of Missouri St. Louis, the school that owns the station. But an untold story lies beneath recommendations such as the one written for Wente. Despite the growth of membership under Wente's management, the university terminated her position following an investigation of the station's finances. The recommendation that Wente received from the university reportedly was written as part of a settlement in which the school allowed Wente to resign rather than be fired.

The growth in membership under Wente's management is mentioned in the letter, but no mention of the other terms of the settlement is made in the recommendation.[59] For example, the settlement required that Wente never again seek employment with the university. After leaving KWMU, Wente started her own fundraising company and reportedly has worked with radio stations in New York, Denver, Chicago, and Washington. Regardless of what actually occurred between the university and Wente, and who the villains and victims are in this story, the university's full assessment of Wente was not present in her recommendation.

Such stories are not meant to illustrate that settlement and severance agreements are bad and should be eliminated or that people receiving recommendations in this manner are bad employees or that the financial and emotional cost savings negotiated through such processes are not meaningful. Even so, a clear reality is that settlement agreements and severances are vehicles that perpetuate the use of the unreliable recommendation system.

Chapter Ten

Recommendation Intoxication and the Erosion of Academic Excellence

Each year, in an effort to select smart and well-rounded candidates, admissions officers in academic institutions across the nation review thousands of application portfolios. They scan test scores, personal essays, and *recommendations* looking for evidence that applicants will succeed in an academic environment, become productive workers, and return to schools with generous financial donations. For schools, these applicants are one-part scholarly future and one-part business investment.

The competition to become a scholar and business investment, particularly at Ivy League schools, is fierce. For example, only about 10 percent of the approximately 200,000 applicants who sought admission to an "Ivy 8" school were admitted to the class of 2013.[60]

Recommendations play a significant role in this selection process. However, the weight assigned to recommendations varies from school to school. Studies show that test scores, grades, and curriculum are typically the primary admissions criteria, but recommendations are also considered.[61]

A closer look, however, reveals that the importance placed on recommendations in the academic environment is misguided. In fact, the recommendation tradition is eroding academic excellence. The following situations reveal the road blocks to using recommendations in the academic world. These situations show how the recommendation process pressures applicants to relinquish power over their academic and professional futures. Further, these situations highlight the troubling shift in values away from academic excellence toward an emphasis on marketing. This trend is unhealthy because academic institutions produce the workplace leaders of tomorrow.

Road Block – My Way or the Highway

When Micah Spradling, a twenty-two-year-old Texas Tech student, enrolled in Dr. Michael Dini's introductory biology course, he discovered that Dini required students who wanted recommendations to agree with and promote the scientific theory of the origins of man.[62]

Dini, described by some university officials and students as a religious person, reportedly wrote that students who could not agree with and promote the scientific theory of the origins of man could not be effective practitioners in a field based on biology.[63] Dini also said his policy was not intended to discriminate against religious beliefs. Rather, his policy was designed to ensure that the students he recommended were scientists.[64]

Students varied in their opinions of Dini's policy. Some saw no conflict between their own religious beliefs and Dini's policy. Others believed that Dini's policy required students to abandon their belief in creationism.

Spradling was among the camp of students who believed Dini's policy required denial of Christian beliefs. He contacted the Liberty Legal Institute, a Christian lawyer organization, which filed a complaint with the Justice Department alleging religious discrimination. The Justice Department discontinued the investigation after Dini adjusted the wording of his policy to one requiring students to *articulate* rather than *believe* evolutionary theory.[65]

Whether or not this was a case of a loosely worded website or an attack on creationist beliefs, the Dini-Spradling conflict shows how recommendations, even in a setting that encourages freedom of expression, can become leverage that manipulates students based on the intentional or unintentional motives of the recommender.

While this case had a workable outcome for Dini and Spradling, other students who disagreed with the policy may have dropped the course, changed professors, or transferred to other universities. Still others simply may have lied to secure recommendations. The line between the use of recommendations to advance professional and personal beliefs is thin. Obviously professors who would use recommendations to advance personal beliefs make unreliable assessments. The recommendations resulting from such situations illustrate an inappropriate use of power rather than a description of student skill and intellect.

Road Block – Hear No Evil See No Evil

Another weakness of the recommendation system in the academic world is the fact that students routinely waive their rights to see the contents of recommendations. Many application forms include sections where students can opt-in or opt-out of reading recommendations written about them. Students tend to opt-out because they do not want to appear to be distrustful of recommenders, and they fear that opting-in gives the appearance that they have something to hide. Some recommenders report that such confidentiality allows them to be more candid in their assessments.

This layer of secrecy prevents students from reviewing and challenging damaging discrepancies.

As an example of the pitfalls of waivers, consider the following excerpt from a recommendation reportedly written in support of an applicant to Kenyon College. The recommender described the student as a person who "travels to the beat of his own drum. I'd tell you what the drum says, but I can't hear it. Not many can...He'll be that guy hanging around the lab eating a cheese sandwich and telling a joke that only he will get..."[66]

These comments may have been a case of humor gone awry, an honest assessment, or a pointed attempt to disparage the applicant. In any case, the admissions officer reported that the comments contributed to the student being placed on the waitlist.

Had this student reviewed the recommendation, he likely would not have included it in his application file, unless the ability to eat cheese sandwiches was a requirement for admission. Further, had the professor known the student would see the recommendation, he likely would have limited his comments to skill sets directly related to potential for academic success instead of sandwich preferences.

The cloak of confidentiality provides entry to other flaws, such as forgeries. For example, the Pomona College dean of admissions, in a 2005 interview, recalled an incident where three students from the same high school applied for admission. A parent of one of the students, in an apparent effort to minimize the competition, was believed to have forged negative recommendations about the other two applicants. The admissions counselor suspected something was amiss and contacted the high school. The high school personnel involved were very upset by these negative recommendations. Because the admissions counselor suspected the forgeries and investigated further, the disparaged applicants were admitted to Pomona, and the applicant suspected of the forgery was denied admission.[67]

But how many admissions counselors are on the lookout for forgeries? Clearly responsibility for investigating discrepancies, from forgeries to misstatements, should not rest solely with admissions officers. Students should be a part of this process by knowing the content of their recommendations.

Road Block – Self-Marketing

Adding to the mix of evolution vs. creation, cheese sandwiches, and parental sabotage is the academic world's increasing focus on self-marketing. Self-marketing has become a skill applicants must master. And reportedly some 5,000 admissions consulting businesses have stepped in to help students in this process.[68]

Consider this promotional statement made by "The Ivy Coach," (http://www.theivycoach.com) an independent college admissions consultant company. The importance of self-marketing is stressed on the company's website:

"As colleges become more competitive, prospective students need to develop special talents, skills, and experiences to gain admission from their top college choices. Yet having those talents, skills, and experiences still may not be enough. Students need to market their specialty wisely as they search for the college that is right for them."[69]

The same website describes one of the coaching services it offers to help students with recommendations:

"...We discuss which teachers to ask for letters of recommendation and coach our students on how to 'impress' their teachers and their guidance counselor, so that their letters will eventually impress admissions counselors..."[70]

Not everyone, however, has the financial resources to pay for a college admissions coach. Coaching businesses often charge hefty fees, going as high as $15,000 to $40,000 for their consulting packages.[71] Applicants on more limited budgets may elect to consult books on the subject. For example, the book *Ivy League Reference Letters: 30 Successful Law School Recommendations* features sample letters likely to be viewed favorably by admissions officers.

In a competitive environment, a certain amount of self-marketing is necessary, but the emphasis on self-marketing creates two problems. First, it encourages the pursuit of an impressive appearance *for the sole purpose of getting a good recommendation*. This comes at the expense of pursuing scholastic excellence and academic relationships for their intellectual value. This is not to say that admissions consultants are bad or should not be used, particularly those who stress talents, skills, and experiences, but the current emphasis on marketing in the academic world encourages the *good face* dependency that leads to poor business decisions in the workplace.

Secondly, when everyone uses a coach or a book on how to write "glowing" recommendations, such recommendations are rendered meaningless because they cannot be distinguished from all the other "glowing" recommendations.[72]

Why does this *recommendation inflation* occur?

Many teachers and professors hesitate to criticize students. Some report that their goal is to help students get into academic institutions, not to be critics.[73] Others do not write negative recommendations because they have been counseled to eliminate comments that expose them to lawsuits. Consequently, admissions officers tend to receive positive recommendations. When all students are outstanding—and they are according to the recommenders in this situation—the system fails.

Road Block – Parental Meddling

Yet another flaw that results in meaningless information is an activity called "parental meddling." In this situation, parents, eager to get their children into the best schools engage in "teacher shopping." "Teacher shopping" occurs when parents ask several teachers to provide recommendations for their children. Parents review and then select the best recommendations to include in the student's application packet for admission to schools.[74]

Road Block – The Memory Challenged Recommender
The value of recommendations is eroded further when recommenders, some responsible for teaching hundreds of students each year, simply do not remember the students requesting recommendations. Enter the *generic* recommendation. A generic recommendation is one that is pre-written and includes general skills and traits that could be possessed by any applicant. Some recommenders keep generic recommendations on file for such situations. For example, some recommenders keep on file three types of recommendations—one describing a *star* applicant, one describing a *good or average* applicant, and a third describing a *less than average or poor performer*. Such recommenders simply select the generic letter they wish to use and fill in the applicant's name in the appropriate places.

Road Block – The Time and Energy Challenged Recommender
Other recommenders forego writing letters altogether. Claiming that they are too busy to draft letters, they ask students to write their own recommendations. The recommender then reviews the letters, copies them on letterhead, and signs them. Letters written by students reflect

a recommender's *agreement* not the recommender's own assessment. Although such recommenders often claim that this practice helps students reflect upon and identify their own strengths and weaknesses, the content of such letters actually reflect a student's mastery of self-promotion.

If recommendations in the admission process are unreliable, why do academic institutions use them?

They do so because the reliability of test scores as the major indicator of success in academic environments has been challenged. The affirmative action debate illuminates one reason for continuing the recommendation tradition. One argument in support of affirmative action is that recommendations are as predictive of success as test scores. Regardless of the final outcome of the ongoing affirmative action debate, the flawed nature of recommendations must be addressed in the academic process.

Chapter Eleven

When Recommendation Intoxication Marries Technology

In May 2003, the popular professional social networking site LinkedIn was launched, changing the way millions of people approach networking and business contacts. With an estimated $100 million in revenue in 2008 and as many as 40 million users, the site has revolutionized the way the workplace communicates.[75]

LinkedIn allows people to expand their professional networks by sharing contacts in an online environment. Professionals from all industries have eagerly joined the LinkedIn network, often before understanding the benefits and costs of being connected to others in this manner.

LinkedIn Recommendations

LinkedIn allows people to request and to receive recommendations. Requesters may seek recommendations by: 1) sending bulk e-mails to their contacts, 2) sending an individual e-mail to an individual contact, or 3) providing a recommendation and receiving a reciprocal recommendation.[76] The marriage of professional networking technology to the recommendation tradition has created concerns. Such concerns recently became a hot topic among LinkedIn users and with bloggers who, to their credit, have actively identified flaws in the system and suggested solutions. The flaws they have identified are on target, but the solutions, unfortunately, miss the mark.

The problem?

Their solutions are based on the assumption that the recommendation system should exist at all, when in fact the system should be discarded. Consider the following concerns raised by professionals in online discussions focusing on this topic.[77]

The bulk recommendation request flaw

Many LinkedIn users question the practice of requesting recommendations in bulk. A bulk e-mail is one sent to all people on a LinkedIn user's contact list rather than to just one contact. Critics of the bulk e-mail practice believe recommendations should be requested only from recommenders who have detailed knowledge of the requester's work and character. Such professionals rightly question the value of recommendations from people who may have only a distant relationship with the requester. Many who take this view believe people should request recommendations offline, request recommendations by individual e-mail, or wait for an unsolicited recommendation.

The prolific recommender flaw

Reportedly, some LinkedIn users are prolific recommenders, providing recommendations to all in their network. Critics of this practice believe such an approach weakens the value of recommendations posted on LinkedIn because everyone receives the same "good" recommendation. These critics suggest that recommenders choose a few star performers and provide recommendations only for those people.[78]

The reviewing the recommender flaw

Another criticism of LinkedIn recommendations is that requesters may preview and reject recommendations before the comments are published on their profile pages. This feature is criticized by some recommenders who believe that the people they are recommending should not have the option to accept or reject comments, thereby selecting only the "best" recommendations. However, this feature is a strength rather than a weakness. Requesters should have knowledge of comments made by recommenders and the ability to review information for appropriateness and accuracy.

The public forum flaw

One critic rightly noted that recommenders tend to make overly positive rather than accurate comments because LinkedIn recommendations are viewed by others in the network.[79]

The focus on technology flaw

Clearly these criticisms of LinkedIn recommendations focus on flaws in the technology, not flaws in the recommendation system. For example, critics have suggested eliminating the "request a recommendation" feature in order to solve the mass e-mail request problem. But even if the technology were adjusted, the recommendation tradition is unreliable—online or on paper. Any reliance on the recommendation system, no matter what the medium, is irreparably flawed. For example, the same "no recommendations" approach employers use in the brick-and-mortar world is now being advanced as an appropriate approach in the LinkedIn world to shield employers from litigation.[80]

But curiously, critics of LinkedIn recommendations are careful not to criticize the recommendation tradition. In fact, most clearly state that they believe recommendations are an important source of information about an applicant's professional reputation. And some state emphatically that the notion of eliminating recommendations is misguided or just plain ridiculous. But this dogmatic adherence to tradition is the result of recommendation intoxication and is a big mistake. Reputation, expressed through the lens of the flawed recommendation system, is not a reliable assessment tool. The exploration of assessment tools capable of improving workplace success must be continued.

The point here is not to condemn LinkedIn or the concept of growing one's professional contacts. However, caution is in order when applying a questionable assessment tool (the recommendation system) to a new and powerful technology. The costs must be considered.

Adding technology to the continued use of recommendations further entrenches the workplace in the precarious pattern of relying on an intoxicating but unreliable habit to make decisions. In this instance, the marriage of technology to the recommendation tradition is not a worthy union.

Chapter Twelve:

Speaking Truth to Intoxication

We are a nation of creative thinkers prone to dreaming up all sorts of arguments to support the status quo. And when it comes to recommendation intoxication, this is certainly true.

Recommendations have been part of human culture for a long time. Even the Bible speaks of recommendation use.[81] And as with other long-standing traditions, we have come up with several creative arguments for keeping this intoxicating albeit unreliable system in place. But for every point in support of staying intoxicated, a compelling counterpoint exists:

- **Point:** Recommendations are important.
  Counterpoint: Recommendations are important only because, as a society, we have agreed to adhere to this unreliable system of assessment.

- **Point:** Professional reputation is important.
  Counterpoint: It is critical to recognize that discerning how people are *regarded* and how they *are* involves two different processes. Employers must concentrate less on reputation, which can be gamed or sabotaged, and more on details that can be verified—degrees, criminal background, and work product. Emphasis on reputation alone is irresponsible and financially destructive.

- **Point:** Most people are hired on the basis of recommendations, and the workplace continues to function.
  Counterpoint: In fact, the workplace is not reaching its full potential under the current system. This is due in large part to the inaccuracy of the recommendation system.

- **Point:** The recommendation system prevents violence in the workplace.
  Counterpoint: Clearly, people who commit violent acts in the workplace are indeed hired under the recommendation system.

- **Point:** Abandoning the status quo will push the recommendation system farther underground. People talk. Admissions and hiring professionals will get information about potential employees on the "down-low."

  Counterpoint: Admissions and hiring professionals who get information on the "down-low" will jeopardize their financial potential. Individuals engaging in this practice will do so knowing that they are receiving unreliable information—a waste of time and money. Abandoning the unreliable recommendation system will inspire decision makers to conduct thorough inquiries using more reliable assessment and verification techniques. Further, decision makers will be forced to follow their own good sense rather than trusting in a *good face* or an inaccurate positive (or negative) recommendation.

Chapter Thirteen

Kicking the Habit

Fear of letting go of a longstanding, seemingly well-regarded tradition is a daunting proposition, particularly because recommendation intoxication makes the workplace feel good—safer, more productive, and more structured. Steeped in the recommendation tradition, we rightfully require more evidence than mere garden-variety office stories to recognize the unreliable nature of recommendations and to change course. Enter the recommendation experts.

Consider the conclusions of recent studies examining the recommendation system:

- Hiring professionals and academic admissions officers recognize that the recommendation system is flawed.
- A significant number of non-academic professionals believe that recommendations have limited value and that their use could be discontinued.

- Academic professionals are less inclined to abandon the recommendation system; however, many criticize the system and question its value.
- Experts recommend more research on the topic before recommendations "...become an entirely useless, biased, and invalid selection tool..."[82]

  Further, experts caution that the continued use of recommendations requires more research to "investigate what specific contribution they make to the selection process and how to improve this contribution..."[83]

The body of evidence shows that the workplace cannot trust its financial future to the intoxicating but unreliable recommendation system. So what can we do about it? What steps must the workplace take to kick the recommendation intoxication habit and right its course?

What Employers Can Do

The current recommendation system weakens the financial potential of every business. Employers must move into the twenty-first century by adopting a *new business model* that does not include the unreliable recommendation system.

The new model would ensure that employers conduct the necessary background investigation to discover criminal activity and the revocation of licenses.

The new model would encourage hiring professionals to abandon the "good face is a letter of recommendation" habit that the workplace has relied on to its detriment.

The new model would put the power of selecting, promoting, and keeping good employees in the hands of executives, hiring professionals, and job applicants rather than in the hands of middle-management gatekeepers.

The new model would alleviate potential avenues for lawsuits.

The new model would force more attention to detail during the interview stage of job candidate assessment.

What Employees and Job Applicants Can Do

The current recommendation system weakens the professional integrity of every professional person. Employees must empower themselves and protect their professionalism by embracing the new model.

The new model means that job applicants should opt out of employment with companies that require recommendations, particularly when those same companies refuse to provide this service to outgoing employees. When all job seekers do this, employers will be motivated to change their reliance on recommendations.

What Academic Institutions Can Do

The admissions process must be focused more on genuine talent and less on personal branding. This can be accomplished in part by adopting the new model.

The new model means actively questioning the current focus on marketing rather than scholastic excellence.

The new model requires active and continued dialogue about the criteria for admissions, including the pros and cons of recommendations.

The new model requires continued research on the specific benefits recommendations provide if their use is to be continued.

What Students Can Do

The recommendation process threatens the integrity of students' academic achievement and professional success.

The new model requires that students routinely inspect the contents of recommendations written about them. In fact, some universities have open records policies that allow students to do this. What students do not know can and does hurt them.

The new model requires students to consider the risks of working for employers who require applicants to provide recommendations, particularly those who refuse to provide recommendations for their outgoing employees.

The new model means students would be wise to consider employment in industries where their work product *is* their recommendation rather than assessment by middle-manager gatekeepers.

The new model means students must think creatively about their professional futures and consider self-employment as one means of breaking the stranglehold that recommendations have on their professional lives.

A Workplace Without Recommendation Intoxication

A workplace without recommendations may seem far-fetched, silly, or even appalling. But keep in mind that such attitudes are actually a form of denial that a problem exists. This tour of workplace stories and research has shown that our dependency on recommendations has real and costly pitfalls.

The human brain may be wired to become beguiled by and to engage in addictive behaviors—to seek gossip in the form of recommendations in order to feel confident about who we employ, who we promote, and who we trust with our money. But human beings also have the capacity to recognize the costs of such behavior and change course. Our reliance on recommendations is an addiction, a habit steeped in tradition that we engage in without much thought. But a closer look at the impact of the recommendation system on the workplace reveals that a *new model* is long overdue. It's time to kick the recommendation habit and abandon intoxication in favor of a new model for a successful workplace.

Endnotes

Chapter 1:

1

A variety of sources were consulted to reconstruct and verify the facts of the arrest of Dr. Ray Mettetal, which was later determined to be illegal. Sources included but were not limited to "Murder Charge for Doctor," (National Desk), *New York Times*, August 29, 1995; "Critics Call Medical Board 'Too Lenient': NC5 Investigates Consumer Alert," *NewsChannel5.com*, February 22, 2007, http://www.newschannel5.com/global/story.asp?s=612341 3&ClientType=Printable (accessed on July 3, 2009).

2

David Rock, "Why Millions of Brains Love (and Hate) Twitter," *Psychology Today*, September 27, 2009, http://www.psychologytoday.com/blog/your-brain-work/200909/why-millions-brains-love-and-hate-twitter

Chapter 2:

3

United States Dept. of Labor Bureau of Labor Statistics. "The Employment Situation" *News*. USDL 09-0482, May 8, 2009. Web

Chapter 3:

4

"Madoff's Victims," *Wall Street Journal*, March 6, 2009 (last update), http://s.wsj.net/public/resources/documents/st_madoff_victims_20081215.html (accessed on March 6, 2009).

5

FINRA, "Avoiding Investment Scams" www.finra.org © 2010 FINRA. All rights reserved. FINRA is a registered trademark of the Financial Industry Regulatory Authority, Inc. Reprinted with permission from FINRA.

6

Nouriel Roubini, "United States of Ponzi, Doctor Doom," *Forbes.com*, March 3, 2009, (accessed on August 16, 2009).

7

John Kenneth Galbraith, introduction to *Krueger Genius and Swindler*, 1ˢᵗ ed., by Robert Shaplen (Alfred A. Knopf, Borzoi Books, 1960).
The original text states:
"...first of all, there is a tendency to confuse good manners, good tailoring and, above all, an impressive bearing and speech with integrity and intelligence..."

8

U.S. Department of Labor, *Handbook of Labor Statistics* (1973).

9

"A Letter of Recommendation: How Dr. Fowler Was Swindled By An Amanuensis—A Clever Forgery," *New York Times,* February 17, 1879.

10

For a more in-depth explanation of commodities futures trading see National Futures Association, "Opportunity and Risk: An Educational Guide to Trading Futures and Options on Futures," National Futures Association, 2006, http://www.nfa.futures.org/-NFA-investor-information/ publication-library/-opportunity-and-risk-entire.pdf.

11

Neptuno Treuhand- und Verwaltungsgesellschaft, MBH and FESAG Financial Engineering Services, GMBH v. Patrick H. Arbor and Chicago Board of Trade. No.1-95-1894 (Ill. Ct. Op. 6th Div. March 13, 1998).

Chapter 4:

12

Garcia Lily (quoting anon. letter), "It's a Fool's Errand to Try and Correct an Egoistic Boss," *Washingtonpost.com*, May 14, 2009, (accessed on May 14, 2009).

13

WBI and Zogby, 2007 WBI-Zogby U.S. Survey, (WBI and Zogby 2007), http://workplacebullying.org/research/WBI-Zogby2007Survey.html

14

Beverly Kaye and Sharon Jordan-Evans, *Love 'em or Lose 'em: Getting Good People to Stay,* 4th ed. (San Francisco, Berrett-Koehler Publishers, Inc. 2008) citing Saratoga Institute California study (2000).

15

For a more in-depth description of this see Beverly Kaye and Sharon Jordan-Evans, *Love 'em or Lose 'em: Getting Good People to Stay,* 4th ed. (San Francisco, Berrett-Koehler Publishers, Inc. 2008): 134.

16

Jenny Cromie, "Workplace Bullying Can Cost You," *Great Lakes HR Now WWJ 950 Radio,* May 2, 2007, featured on the Workplace Bullying Institute website, www.workplacebullying.org/press/glhrn050207.html

17

Diane Cadrain, "Job detectives dig deep for defamation," *HR Magazine,* October 2004.

18
Ibid.

19

U.S. Equal Employment Opportunity Commission, Sexual Harassment Charges EEOC and FEPAs Combined: FY 1997–FY 2009, *sexual harassment table, http://www.eeoc.gov/ eeoc/statistics/enforcement/sexual_harassment.cfm* (accessed on November 7, 2010).

Chapter 5:

20

Randi W. v. Muroc Joint Unified School District, 929 P. 2d 582 (Cal. 1997).

21

Robinson v. Shell Oil Company 519 U.S. 337 (1997); U.S. Equal Employment Opportunity Commission, "Milestones in the History of the U.S. Equal Employment Opportunity Commission: 1990," U.S. Equal Employment Opportunity Commission, http://www.eeoc.gove/abouteeoc/35th/milestones/1990. html (accessed on June 21, 2009); see also Title VII of the Civil Rights Act of 1964.

22

Jerner v. Allstate Insurance Company No. 93-09472 (Fla. Cir. Ct. August 10, 1995).
This is an unpublished opinion. The citation was located through a secondary source and a description of the case through news and law review articles including: Marianne

Jennings, *Business: Its Legal, Ethical and Global Environment,* 8th ed. (Cengage Learning 2009): 299; see also Julie N. Lynem, "Lawsuits keep bosses mum on references," *San Diego Union-Tribune,* September 10, 2001. E1; Alfred G. Haggerty, "Ex-Fireman's Fund Employee Kills Three Executives," *National Underwriter Property and Casualty-Risk and Benefits Management,* February 8, 1993.

23
According to the most current survey conducted by the Society for Human Resource Management, 54 percent of employers say they have a policy prohibiting references or disclosure of information about current and former employees.
Mary Elizabeth Burke, *2004 Reference and Background Checking Survey Report,* (Alexandria, VA, Society for Human Resource Management, January 2005): 17 fig. 9.

This is so even though reportedly more than half of the U.S. states have adopted "employer immunity" or "reference immunity" statutes that offer some protection to employers who share information about former employees. These laws do not require employers to provide references, but encourage them to share information. The statutes vary in level of protection for employers, and some have come under criticism for a variety of reasons.

For a partial summary of such statutes and a description of some of the criticisms see Markita Cooper, "Job Reference

Immunity Statutes: Prevalent But Irrelevant," 11 Cornell L.J. & Pub. Pol'y 1 (2001): 40–41, 44–46, 60–66.

The idea behind such laws is to promote the free flow of information in order to decrease incompetence and violence in the workplace; however, more than half of employers surveyed report that they still do not provide references. Some believe this reticence to provide information actually increases exposure to lawsuits based on negligence and suggest that it is better for employers to document and share information about former employees freely. Such critics predict that if employers do not change their course on this, the law will force changes by making disclosure mandatory.

24
This trend has been widely discussed in the legal community. For more information see Markita Cooper, "Job Reference Immunity Statutes: Prevalent But Irrelevant," 11 Cornell L.J. & Pub. Pol'y 1 (2001): 1–15, 40–41, 44–46, 60–66; Matthew W. Finkin and Kenneth G. Dau-Schmidt, "Solving the Employee Reference Problem: Lessons From the German Experience," 57 *Am. J. Comp. L.* 387 (2009); Julie N. Lynem, "Lawsuits keep bosses mum on references," *San Diego Union-Tribune,* September 10, 2001: E1.

25
Mary Elizabeth Burke, *2004 Reference and Background Checking Survey Report*, (Alexandria, VA, Society for Human Resource Management, January 2005): 3.

Chapter 6:

26

U.S. Bureau of Labor Statistics, U.S. Department of Labor, 2010, "Four most frequent work- related fatal injury events, 1992-2009," http://www.bls.gov/iif/oshwc/cfoi/cfch0008.pdf (accessed on January 24, 2011).

Chapter 7:

27

Anne VanderMey, "MBA Application Letters: Who to Ask," *Business Week online*, February 24, 2009: 3.

28

Ibid.

29

Scholars Trix and Psenka, in their article "Exploring the Color of Glass" referred to such irrelevant comments as "doubt raisers." Such doubt raisers can harm applicants because they are so irrelevant that it gives the appearance that the recommender could find nothing else meritorious about the candidate to write about. Frances Trix and Carolyn Psenka, "Exploring the Color of Glass: letters of recommendation for female and male medical faculty," *Discourse and Society* 14(2) (2003):191–220: 202.

30

A small number of these results were dictionaries, thesauri, and medical reference books.

Google searched on September 8, 2009. In 2011, this number rose to 2,320,000.

31

Mary Elizabeth Burke, *2004 Reference and Background Checking Survey Report,* (Alexandria, VA, Society for Human Resource Management, January 2005): viii.

32

Michael G. Aamodt and Naceema Thompson, "Employment References: Who Are We Talking About?" Paper presented at the annual meeting of the International Personnel Management Association Assessment Council, Chicago, Illinois, June 22, 1998.

33

John Ashbury, "Letter to the Editor," *Chicago Review*, Summer 2008, 53.4: 356.

34
Ibid.

35

An estimated 20 percent of people have used prescription drugs for nonmedical purposes during their lives, and 54 percent of people drink coffee on a daily basis. For more information see National Institute on Drug Abuse Research Report Series, "Prescription Drugs: Abuse and Addiciton" Revised 2005, http://www.nida.nih.gov/ResearchReports/Prescription/Prescription.html; National Coffee Association website, http://www.ncausa.org/i4a/pages/index.cfm?pageid=1

36

The names of the people have been changed to protect privacy.

37

Frances Trix and Carolyn Psenka, "Exploring the Color of Glass: letters of recommendation for female and male medical faculty," *Discourse and Society* 14(2) (2003): 191–220: 212.

38

Ibid., 211.

39

The researchers who conducted this study changed specific details to protect the parties involved. The letter writer went on to recommend the candidate "without reservation," but of course the damage made by the inappropriate comments was already done.

Ibid., 205–206.

40
Ibid., 204.

41
Jeffrey H. Greenhaus, Saroj Parasuraman, Wayne M. Wormley, "Effects of Race on Organizational Experiences, Job Performance Evaluations, and Career Outcomes," *Academy of Management Journal* 33(1) (1990): 66.

42
Devon Alfred Bryan, Avon Products Inc. "Differences in Trait Interpretation Between Black and White Professionals When Evaluating Letters of Recommendation," *Applied H.R.M. Research* 3(2) (1992): 130–161:130.

43
Hillary Chura, "Can an Employer's Past Follow its Workers?" *NYTimes.com,* February 22, 2009.

44
Diane Cadrain, "Job detectives dig deep for defamation," *HR Magazine,* October 2004.

Chapter 8:

45
Diane Cadrain, "Job detectives dig deep for defamation," *HR Magazine,* October 2004.

46

Confirmed by e-mail exchange with Documented Reference Check representative on October 15, 2009, 7:13 p.m. (This number includes all reference report types and includes national and international sales.)

47

Allisontaylor.com/negative_bad_references.asp (accessed on October 15, 2009).

48

Diane Cadrain, "Job detectives dig deep for defamation," *HR Magazine,* October 2004; allsiontaylor.com/negative_bad_references.asp (accessed on October 15, 2009).

49

J. Mcknight, V.P. Marketing—quoted on Allison & Taylor Inc. website
Allisontaylor.com/negative_bad_references.asp, (accessed on October 15, 2009).

50

Diane Cadrain, "Job detectives dig deep for defamation," *HR Magazine,* October 2004.

51
Ibid.

52

Documented Reference Check www.badreferences.com (accessed on October 2009).

Chapter 9:

53
Bill Sizemore, "Don't ask, don't tell: Christian Coalition's dismissal of Judy Liebert as the group's chief financial officer," *Church & State*, October 1997, 50. n9.

54
Ibid.

55
APA, "2009 Great Places in America,"
http://www.planning.org/greatplaces/ (accessed on March 8, 2010),
Contact: Online webform through website.

National Trust for Historic Preservation, "2005 Distinctive Destinations,"
http://www.preservationnation.org/travel-and-sites/sites/northeast-region/bath-me-2005.html

56
"Library apologizes for firing librarian: Patten Free Library apologizes for firing Nyree Thomas," *American Libraries,* June–July 2008, 39.6: 34.

57
Emmanuel Okoro v. Marriott International, Inc. and The Ritz Carlton Hotel. S.D.N.Y. 07 Civ. 165 (DLC) Op. and Order.

58

Larry Blaskey, "More charges filed against Watkins," *The Daily Dispatch,* December 6, 2007, www.douglasdispatch. com/articles/2007 (accessed on November 19, 2009).

59

Deb Peterson, "KWMU GM whose firing made waves sails off happy," *St. Louis Post- Dispatch*, November 22, 2008; The Wente Group, http://thewentegroup.com

Chapter 10:

60

Hernandez College consulting and Christian Termont of EERA, "Ivy League Admissions Statistics for Class of 2013," www.hernandezcollegeconsulting.com/ivy-league-admissions-statistics/visited (accessed on November 19, 2009); The Ivy Coach, "2013 Ivy League Admissions Statistics," www.theivycoach.com/class-of-2013-statistics.html.

61

National Association for College Admission Counseling, "2009 State of College Admission Report."

62 –65

The controversial wording of Dr. Dini's website was changed. A variety of sources were consulted to reconstruct the facts of the Dini-Spradling situation, including but not limited to, Associated Press, "Professor's refusal to recommend evolution foes prompts lawsuit, probe," *Associated Press*, January 31, 2003, www.firstamendment-center.org/news.aspx?id=3015; Nick Madigan, "Professor's Snub of Creationists Prompts U.S. Inquiry," *New York Times, Nytimes.com,* February 3, 2003.

66
Alvin P. Sanoff, "A steep road to admission. Letters of recommendation are important in student selection," *USA Today*, December 27, 2005.

67
Ibid.

68
Jacques Steinberg, "Before College, Costly Advice Just on Getting In," *New York Times*, July 19, 2009, vol. CLVIII no. 54,741:1, 4.

69
The Ivy Coach, "Winning at the College Admissions Game,"
http://www.theivycoach.com/talented-high-school-students-winning-at-the-college-admissions-game.html

70
http://www.theivycoach.com/why-hire-an-independent-college-consultant.html

71
Jacques Steinberg, "Before College, Costly Advice Just on Getting In," *New York Times,* July 19, 2009, vol. CLVIII no. 54,741: 1, 4.

72
Glenn C. Altschuler, "COLLEGE PREP; Dear Admissions Committee," *New York Times, Nytimes.com*, January 9, 2000; Jessica M. Nicklin and Sylvia G. Roch, "Letters of Recommendation Controversy and Consensus from Expert Perspectives," *International Journal of Selection and Assessment,* 17(1) (March 2009): 88.

73
Glenn C. Altschuler, "COLLEGE PREP; Dear Admissions Committee," *New York Times, Nytimes.com*, January 9, 2000.

74
Qtg. Lisa McLaughlin, college admissions consultant in Alvin P. Sanoff, "A steep road to admission. Letters of recommendation are important in student selection," *USA Today,* December 27, 2005:1D

Chapter 11:

75
LinkedIn, "Company History," http://press.linkedin.com/history (accessed June 9, 2009). As of January 2011, the LinkedIn website reported approximately 90 million users with about 1

million people joining the site every twelve days. http://press.linkedin.com/about/ (accessed January 28, 2011).

76

Jan Vermeiren, *How to Really use LinkedIn* (United States, Booksurge, 2009): 96, 97; Jason Alba, comment on "I'm On LinkedIn Now What??? The blog behind the book," comment posted on June 11, 2008,
http//imonlinkedinnowwhat.com/2008/06/11/
linkedin-recommendation-thoughts/
(accessed on October 5, 2009).

77

The criticisms of LinkedIn recommendations were compiled from comments posted on blogs including those listed below, but the names of the individual commentators have not been included when it was found that several people, rather than one particular person, had expressed the same or similar ideas.
"I'm On LinkedIn Now What???The blog behind the book,"
http//imonlinkedinnowwhat.com/2008/06/11/
linkedin-recommendation-thoughts/

Adam Nash, comment on "Recommendations and the Reputation Economy," LinkedIn Blog, comment posted on July 23, 2009,
http://blog.linkedin.com/2009/07/23/adam-nash-recommendations-and-the-reputation-economy, (accessed on October 5, 2009).

Jeremiah Owyang, comment on "Requested Recommen-dations on Social Networks: Why I Won't Do It," Web Strategy Blog, comment posted on July 17, 2009, www.web-strategist.com/blog/2009/07/17/ requestedrecommendations_social_networks, (accessed on October 5, 2009).

78
Kenny E. Thomas, comment on "I'm On LinkedIn Now What??? The blog behind the book," LinkedIn Blog, com-ment posted on June 11, 2008, http://imonlinkedinnowwhat.com/2008/06/11/ linkedin-recommendation-thoughts/

79
Jeremiah   Owyang,   comment   on   "Requested Recommendations on Social Networks: Why I Won't Do It," Web Strategy Blog, comment posted on July 17, 2009, www.web-strategist.com/blog/2009/07/17/ requestedrecommendations_social_networks, (accessed on October 5, 2009).

80
Tim Eavenson, comment on "Employers: The LinkedIn Recommendation is Not for You," Current Employment HR Law & Policy Blog, comment posted on July 14, 2009, http://currentemployment.net (accessed on March 2, 2010).

Chapter 12:

81

Holy Bible 2 Corinthians 3:1 (King James Version).

Chapter 13:

82

Jessica M. Nicklin and Sylvia G. Roch, "Letters of Recommendation Controversy and Consensus from Expert Perspectives," *International Journal of Selection and Assessment,* 17(1) (March 2009): 90.

83

Ibid., 88.

Questions for further discussion:

1) Does your employer or school have a recommendations policy? If so, what is it? What protections does it provide for the employer/school? The job applicant/student? Who benefits the most from the current policy?

2) Do you agree with the author that the "recommendation system problem" is in fact a "vetting" problem? If so, why? If not, why?

3) Some academic institutions reportedly allow students to submit statements explaining their lack of recommendations or to comment on points made in recommendations written about them. What are the benefits and the drawbacks of such a policy? Would it be helpful for employers to adopt a similar policy for job applicants? Such a policy assumes that students will review their recommendations. Does this present problems for recommenders?

4) Do "job detectives" hurt or help the workplace? Should employers use them to check their references? Does your opinion depend on whether you are an employer, job applicant, hiring professional, or student?

5) Do you agree that recommendations should not be a part of the academic admissions process? If

academic institutions are the incubators of the future workforce, how does the admissions process influence the culture of this future workforce? If recommendations are to be discarded, what process, if any, should replace their use? If the recommendations system should be kept in place, what changes, if any, should be made to make recommendations in this context more reliable?

6) Do you agree that students should not opt-out of seeing their recommendations? Is confidentiality about information that concerns "the individual" ever justifiable?

7) A 2009 study entitled "Letters of Recommendation Controversy and Consensus from Expert Perspectives" (Nicklin and Roch), showed that hiring professionals who do not work in academic settings more readily accept the idea of abandoning recommendation use than hiring professionals in academic settings. Why do you think this is the case?

8) Is there a special need for recommendations in the academic admissions process? Does the need for assessment, other than standardized test scores, validate the use of the unreliable recommendation system?

9) Given its unreliable nature, is the recommendation system the proper vehicle for reporting violence in the workplace and schools? Does the ability for employers to perform background checks change

your answer? What about incidents of child moles-
tation where parents, reluctant to expose their
children to more trauma, do not bring criminal
charges?

10) Do you agree that gender bias in recommendations harms applicants? What about race or sexual
preference?

11) Do you agree that the recommendation system supports self-promotion at the expense of excellence in
the academic world?

12) Have you ever suspected that a professor or employer
gave you a less than sterling recommendation?
Describe the incident. Was the recommender correct in his or her assessment? If not, what did you
do to remedy the inaccuracy?

13) Who are the stakeholders in the world of recommendation use? Who stands to lose or to gain from
the continuation of the system?

Glossary:

Accurate – Fact based and without error.

Background check – May include verification of criminal records and academic credentials. A recommendation or reference check may be conducted as part of a background check.

Bulk e-mail – An e-mail function that allows one e-mail to be composed and sent to several recipients.

Defamation – A false statement (written or oral) made to at least one other person that harms the reputation of another.

Employment verification – A document or statement that reveals a former employee's name, job title, and dates of employment only.

Invasion of Privacy – The unjustifiable intrusion upon a person's right to privacy.

LinkedIn – A popular social networking site that allows people to expand their professional networks by sharing contacts in an online environment

Negative recommendation – A recommendation that includes objectively or subjectively disparaging comments about a former employee's job performance.

Negligence – The breach of a duty that causes harm and results in damages.

Neutral recommendation – A recommendation that does not include overly positive or negative comments about a former employee.

Nondisparagement clause – A clause that may appear in a severance agreement that prevents an employee from making negative comments about an employer.

Objective – Not influenced by personal feelings or opinions.

Positive recommendation – A recommendation that does not include overly negative comments and focuses on a former employee's positive characteristics.

Reciprocal recommendation – A reciprocal recommendation situation occurs when one person provides a recommendation for another person in exchange for a recommendation.

Recommendation Intoxication – The reliance on recommendations in the workplace to such an extent that the workplace has lost the ability to make well-reasoned decisions regarding employment.

Reference – A person, often a former supervisor or manager, who is willing to provide written or oral recommendations for former employees.

Referrals – The recommendation of the business services provided by one person to another person.

Settlement agreement – A contract that resolves a disagreement between parties in lieu of further litigation.

Severance package – The pay and benefits an employee receives when leaving employment. Severance packages may include a positive letter of recommendation.

The new model – The abandonment of the traditional recommendation system and adoption of more effective ways to evaluate employees.

Vetting – The process of looking into the background of a person to determine his or her character and fitness for political office or employment.

Index

Topics

Acknowledgments

Thank you to everyone who paved the way with expertise, example, insight, or encouragement. Thank you to the journalists and individuals who granted permission for the stories in this book to be told. And a special thanks to the librarians with the Arlington Virginia Public Library and Library of Congress who provided assistance throughout the project.

About the Author

Erin Haggerty is a research and writing consultant based in Arlington, Virginia. She earned her bachelor's degree in communication from Ohio University, her law degree from University of California Los Angeles School of Law and her master's in library and information science from Catholic University of America. She writes about contemporary issues that influence how people work and live. For more information about the book and Erin Haggerty, visit recommendationtoxication.com.